DESMOND EGAN   A CRITICAL STUDY

DESMOND EGAN
a critical study

Brian Arkins

Desmond Egan

(1·4·96 Queens College)

1992
MILESTONE PRESS
Little Rock U.S.A.

MILESTONE BOOKS
8524 Asher Avenue Little Rock Arkansas 77204

FOR DESMOND FENNELL
scriptori tenero, meo sodali

Grateful acknowledgement is made to Desmond Egan for his kind
permission to cite from his poetry and prose.

Mr. Egan would like to acknowledge the invaluable help and
enthusiasm of
Professor Russell Murphy (Editor, *The Yeats/Eliot Review*)
and of Kim Kamberos

Front cover photograph: Liam Lyons

Printed and bound by
The Guernsey Press Co. Ltd, Guernsey, Channel Islands.

CONTENTS

Abbreviations

CP   Desmond Egan, *Collected Poems* (University of Maine 1983/ Newbridge 1984).

Kenner   *Desmond Egan — The Man and his Work*, ed. H. Kenner (Northern Lights, U.S.A. 1990).

PP   Desmond Egan, *Poems For Peace* (Dublin 1986).

SF   Desmond Egan, *A Song For My Father* (Calstock, Cornwall/ Newbridge 1989).

SPr   Desmond Egan, *The Death of Metaphor — Selected Prose* (Gerrards Cross 1990).

Pen   Desmond Egan, *Peninsula* (Newbridge 1992)

Med   Desmond Egan, *Medea* (Laurinburg, U.S.A. 1991)

ONE

Achievement

1

When Desmond Egan's *Collected Poems* received the National Poetry
Foundation of America Award in 1983 — he was the first European to be
so honored — the event clearly established Egan as a major poet,[1] and
suggested that we should ponder upon the dictum of C.F. Terrell, President of that Foundation: 'Desmond Egan will yet be evaluated as Ireland's
greatest modern poet.'[2] Egan has written a truly remarkable number of
brilliant poems — both private and public, local and international, on a
wide variety of themes — poems that will certainly last. Then, booklength
translations of Egan's poetry into French, Italian, Spanish, Greek, Dutch,
Swedish, Hindi and Japanese either have appeared or are about to appear.[3]
In August 1990 he received another accolade when *Desmond Egan—The
Poet and his Work*, edited by Hugh Kenner[4] and featuring articles by an
international line-up of distinguished academics and writers, was published in the U.S.A. and launched at the Yeats/Pound conference at the
University of Maine.

Taking Egan's status as a major poet as a datum, this book will delineate
the nature of his poetic achievement up to 1992. It will eschew the facile
method of devoting a chapter to each volume of poetry in turn in favor of
a thematic approach: after this opening chapter which attempts to outline
Egan's achievement and a second chapter on various backgrounds to his
work, the remaining six chapters will deal with Landscape, Elegy, Love
Poetry, Political Poetry, The Greek Connection, and Landscape into
History. An annotated bibliography will complete the book.[5]

Of what, then, does the corpus consist? Egan's *Collected Poems* of 1984
brought together material from seven earlier volumes: *Midland* (1972),
Leaves (1974), *Siege!* (1976), *Woodcutter* (1978), *Athlone?* (1980),
Snapdragon (1983), and *Seeing Double* (1983). Two further volumes of
poetry are *A Song For My Father* (1989) and *Peninsula* (1992). Egan's
Selected Prose under the title *The Death of Metaphor* came out in 1990
and his translation of Euripides' *Medea* in 1991.

Behind all Egan's work there lies both a piercing intelligence and a
poet's eye for what is crucial: Egan gets to the core of issues, which means,

in terms of poetry, the minimum of anything superfluous, the maximum brevity. Because poetry is, for Egan, a *creation*:

Poetry impinges on people *in a whole way* — the words 'whole' and 'holy' are etymologically cognate — so that in Plato's terms the gap between this material world of sense perception with its manifold inadequacies and the other transcendent world of the Good, where all these inadequacies are resolved, may be bridged by poetry. As you can see, I'm a Platonist![6]

In producing this creation, Egan has moved from an early private pre-occupation with himself walking the Irish Midlands to a far greater involvement with public issues, especially political ones. But even in *Midland* (1972) there were poems about Northern Ireland and among the political poems of *A Song For My Father* there is an elegiac sequence for the poet's father. What we have in Egan, then, is a very satisfying mix of private and public themes, in which each realm receives its proper due.

The progression towards more public issues has not, of course, been simply willed; as Egan states, 'You have to write about what gets under your skin and there is a difference between polemic which is willed and political poetry — with some accent on *poetry* — which comes from a genuine whole involvement, a real feeling.'[7]

Crucial to this shift in emphasis from the private to the public is the volume *Siege!* of 1976, a watershed in Egan's poetry. Learning from Eliot and Pound, Egan here employs epigraphs, an appendix, notes, quotations from other languages (Greek, Italian, Irish, Latin) and a supple form to write about a public issue, the kidnapping of a foreign industrialist by the I.R.A., in an emphatically modernist mode which stresses ambivalence and paradox. *Siege!* then has led him to a considerable amount of political poetry about Ireland, the United States, Germany and, in particular, the Third World in the volumes *Seeing Double* and *A Song For My Father*.

Every theme, of course, demands an appropriate technique: Egan's use of resolutely modernist technique is noteworthy. To begin with, as Peter van de Kamp has observed, 'Like Yeats, Egan writes books rather than individual poems.'[8] This is specially true of volumes such as *Midland*, which concentrates on the theme of the Irish Midlands; *Athlone?*, which deals exclusively with Egan's home town; *Siege!*, entirely devoted to a kidnapping; and *Snapdragon*, a series of love poems. But the dictum can also be applied to other volumes: consider the concentration of the themes of elegy and politics in *Seeing Double* and *A Song For My Father*, and the programmatic positioning of the political poems 'Young Gifted — and

Unemployed' and 'Feed the World' at the beginning and end of the section 'People' in the latter volume.

Egan adopts a number of technical devices that we associate with modern poetry in general and with American poetry in particular (see Chapter Two): no capital letters for the beginnings of lines, as has been conventional; no punctuation; a refusal of rhyme and of the predictable iambic beat; pervasive asyndeton; the subversion of line ends. All of this stresses that if the times are out of joint, so too must the poetry which chronicles them be; a confused and chaotic world cannot be written about in the ordered and structured manner of discursive prose. A good example of this fluid technique is the fine poem 'Sunday evening' (CP 127):

> hands in jeans along Dollymount I don't see
> the slow line of the wave breaking far,
> out under Howth in mist a Tír na nÓg I don't see
> the long strand quiet as another sky
> nor the season the wrack dead things a saturated beam
>
> — but you who are not there
> sitting any more legs crossed on a sand dune
> picking at chips with musical fingers to laugh
> deeper than the wind that *This is LOVE-ly*
> while the sparse grass blows
>
> forever as I pass

One further and crucial technical device, original to Egan and first found in the volume *Seeing Double*, is the employment in the right-hand margin of a sub-text, which interacts with the main text in a variety of ways: 'as parallel or counter-point, as parody or homage to the main poem.'[9]

A good example of this device can be found at the beginning of the poem 'May Day' (CP 199), where the sub-text glosses 'a radio' in the main text:

road cuts into morning a radio	*the Northern Secretary*
the	
smokes clearly out a neighbor window	*Papal*
and the birds have taken over:	*and Poland dying*
our little lad	*day by day by day*
bubbling wild skipping branches above my	
head	

2

For a taste of Egan's work and its characteristic strengths, let us now examine some poems. First, two poems that present us with statements on his view of art ('Introduction' and 'Non symbolist') and next a short summary of his philosophy ('On the need for philosophy').

In the main text of the 'Introduction' to Egan's *Collected Poems* (CP 15),[10] the essential point is that a dog is scavenging relentlessly in the poet's rubbish bin. Since the sub-text gives an account of the poet's early morning, including his breakfast ('delph sound') and since that morning impinges also on the main text — 'music floats from this very study as/his teeth flitter through cellophane' — the inference to be drawn is that the poet must like the dog do the best he can with the untidy material of reality. For just as the poet cannot stop the dog 'scattering the waste on the tarmac,' so is he also unable to cease portraying items of everyday life.

This is not the only way point of resemblance the dog: the dog is part of the landscape of the Midlands — 'becoming one with/that same fieldscape the maybush the/immemorial skies' — just as the poet is in the sub-text of this poem — '*a swift loops two/thoughts*' — and, at considerable length, in the two volumes that immediately succeed the 'Introduction,' *Midland* and *Leaves*. Then just as the dog's union with the world of nature and with time leaves him free to explore large future possibilities, so the poetry, equated with a bird that sings forever, but cannot be seen — '*somewhere unseeable/ a bird sings centuries*' — will spectacularly develop in the volume of poetry that comes next after *Leaves, Siege!*, and advance to further, new themes in *Athlone?* and in subsequent volumes.

The sub-text of the later poem 'Non symbolist' (CP 216-17) presents us with Egan's poetic *credo* in an uncompromising way:

> *I'm browned off with symbolism*
> *as a device I mean: the MIND*
> *doing an interview*
> *shoving its mike down your neck making*
> *some half-baked programme for*
> *a few cuckoo listeners on v.h.f.*
>   *no —*
> *Yeats Mallarmé and Co. you're out the window*
> *for me at least*
> *what we need is wholeness not the splintered*
> *world of broken glasses*
> *we want the real thing ...*

What the poet rejects is the symbolist mode of coming to grips with things in an oblique way, as in 19th century French poets like Mallarmé,[11] whose theory of transcendental symbolism cut himself off from all contact with reality, and as in Yeats,[12] whose symbolism derives in part from Mallarmé, as mediated through Arthur Symons' book *The Symbolist Movement in Literature*.[13] This device is regarded as too cerebral, too removed from everyday experience, too taken with the inadequacy of the world, and consequently listened to only by an élite. Instead, what Egan commends is a wholeness akin to Jungian integration. So the essential *quidditas* of the apple or a cup of tea, familiar but always new, secular but sacred, is the proper topic for poetry.

While 'Introduction' deals obliquely and 'Non symbolist' directly, with the poet's art, the viewpoint that lies behind that art is presented in the poem 'On the need for philosophy' (CP 213):

even the lovely fierceness
that music which squeezes us whole *frost ivy inside the window*
climbs with the purity of light upwards
as sharply leaves us a *of a sky blue as ice*
dancefloor empty with chairs

sweetpapers *fire bubbles and*
a spider of silence
the huge silent speakers *floats across our cold*

Human beings experience moments of intense passion: Blake's pulsation of the artery, Pater's privileged moment, Joyce's epiphany — but (as we all know to our cost) such moments do not last and it is not long until the dance floor is deserted, the music silent, the chairs empty, the floor littered. The inference to be drawn is in the poem's title 'On the need for philosophy': it is not enough to enjoy special moments; we need a metaphysic, a spiritually satisfying vision of the human condition to enable us to put up with life. What that account might be is richly provided in the poetry of Desmond Egan.

Let us conclude by examining three crucial poems, chosen respectively, from early, middle and late volumes, 'Requiem,', 'V —,' and 'Needing the sea.'

What look like simple poems are by no means as naive as they first appear. Take 'Requiem,' from Egan's second volume *Leaves*, for example. To be read in the general context of a love affair that has come to an end, the four-line 'poem' is a minor *tour de force* (CP 77):

> music you loved has filled like autumn with sadness
> and places we used to be I can hardly bear
> flowers are less than flowers days are of-darkness
> something fell like a leaf when you went away

The crucial technique, as so often in Egan, is that of asyndeton: the omission of connecting particles such as 'and' or 'but' that belong to prose. There is only one 'and' to link the five basic statements of the poem and this joins together two of the key things the lovers shared in the past, music they listened to together and places they frequented together. Again, the use of pronouns is very significant. The second person singular referring to the woman occurs only at the beginning and end of the poem to give us the collocation 'music you loved' and 'you went away,' partnership followed by desertion, involvement with something definite and worthwhile followed by non-involvement, *tout court*. Furthermore, 'you' first becomes 'we' which is then reduced to 'I' before finally turning into 'you' again, but now with a different nuance, an objectified 'you' as against its intimacy of its pronoun in line 1.

Thematically, the poem is equally rich. Autumn functions, as in Horace's *Odes*, as a metaphor for the end of love.[14] Consequently, the music the women loved is equated directly with autumn, no longer heard against the background of a flourishing relationship, but against that of withering loss. Similarly, the places the loves frequented have lost their magic, have become unpleasant and almost unbearable. Again, the omission of relative pronouns in these first two lines is significant. In the phrase 'music you loved' the obvious meaning is made fully explicit by inserting the relative pronoun 'which' after 'music,' but the whole rhythm of the poem suggests the other more allusive reading which has 'music' as subject and 'you' as object: which by equating the two words stresses the woman's love of music. The omission of 'in which' or 'where' in the phrase 'places we used to be' leads to a complex set of meanings: on the one hand, the verb has the connotation of being really alive; on the other, there is an equation between the places and the lovers.

Coming to lines 3-4, we find that the flowers of spring and summer are now dead in the autumn, that the bright days that characterize spring and summer make way for the long evenings of autumn and winter, a point neatly emphasized by the phrase 'of-darkness,' where the preposition is directly linked to the abstract noun 'darkness' by the only piece of punctuation in the entire poem. In the final line, after the very definite statements about music, places, flowers and days, we have a very indefinite 'something' and a very non-specific 'you went away.' The sense of loss is so overwhelming that it cannot be fully articulated, but can only be compared to something else, the falling leaf of autumn, and the woman is now seen not as a frequenter of specific places, but simply as being somewhere else.

Two final points about meter and title. The poem's meter avoids iambic banality by having three of its four lines begin with a trochee and by using a generous number of trisyllablic feet. The poem's title, the accusative singular of the Latin noun *requies*, obviously suggests an elegiac note because of its use as shorthand for the phrase *requiem aeternam dona eis, domine* in the Introit of the Mass for the Dead, but more specifically, through its secondary meaning of 'any dirge or solemn chant for the repose of the dead,'[15] indicates that love has been replaced by the death of love.

A love poem to Egan's wife Vivienne, 'V —' (CP 131) constitutes that quintessential contemporary form of writing, a poem about not being able to write a poem. The intense involvement of the poet in the situation is indicated by the use of the personal pronoun for the first person, 'I,' no fewer than 13 times in the 23 line poem; whereas the personal pronoun for the second person, 'you,' occurs only twice. The result is that, even though 'I' at the beginning of the first line and 'you' at the end of the last bracket the entire poem, the stress is almost entirely on the difficulty of what the poet is trying to do.

The majority of these first person pronouns deal with non-actions, with what the poet will *not* do. He will not get bogged down by the ordinary distractions of a writer's life:

> I will not answer the letter I must answer
> nor lift any phone nor read nor open the hollow door
> not even if the world I love shout
> I will switch on no transistor
> but extravagantly crumble the tooth pages into my basket

What he will do is concentrate exclusively on writing a poem. This process demands introspection, enormous initial concentration on the blank sheet of paper (a feeling known to every writer), the capacity to throw hard-won pages coolly, detachably, into the waste paper basket, the ability to write, as we assume Shakespeare did, primarily for himself. But all this tremendous effort may result in failure: plenty is written, but it is of no consequence, because the writing game is fraught with waste, involves taking risks.

In this situation the poet, though disappointed, does not propose to defend himself or make excuses, for even if no poem results, he has laboured long and hard. And paradoxically, the elaborate catalogue of things the poet will not do have became this poem 'V —,' a successful poem about the failure to write a successful poem.

In contrast with both 'Requiem' and 'V —,' the magnificent opening poem of the volume *Seeing Double* (1983), 'Needing the sea' (CP 185-86), demonstrates the later Egan's preoccupation with public themes. But at the same time the poet's private needs are also chronicled, with the result that we have an apparent clash between the two forces and a poem that is programmatic, since *Seeing Double* as a whole is both public and private.

The initial private section seizes on the title of the poem, 'Needing the sea,' and locates that need in early autumn, in the month of September. Satisfying as the landscape of the Irish Midlands is, when the flowering of summer has come to an end, when falling leaves herald the barrenness of winter, and when the poet himself experiences that barrenness, he seeks out the eternal, spiritual element of the sea, which is opposed to the earth. But this is no mere private whim, since what the poet craves, Kavanagh-like,[16] is the redemptive power of water, something that is sacred, a kind of baptism:

> in September maybe most that time
> when the earth begins to take over again
> something in me gets bogged down and
> cries out for the grace of water

But this basic need is no sooner articulated than he feels an objection coming from somebody who, alert to the sufferings of millions of people in the world, regards such a private need as pure luxury. An objection accepted by the poet as powerful since 19 lines of the 37 line poem are devoted to it. These 19 lines present a damning catalogue of the world's problems: a world economic system which sees billions spent on arms while millions of people in the Third World starve; military dictatorships of whatever political hue that engage in torture and genocide; the struggle for freedom of a country like Poland. All of these phenomena are so essentially dehumanizing that even to think of them 'becomes a kind of dying.'

Nor is Ireland exempt. In Northern Ireland, an innocent man caught up in sectarian violence has his cottage burnt down (cf. the poem 'Hitchhiker,' dealt with in Chapter Six). Down in the Republic a radically unjust system results in massive poverty and unemployment, which leads inevitably to crime and violence, especially in urban areas:

> we all know about the houses of hopes blown up blown out
> we all bump into the local alcos the druggie
> youngsters their adult faces mugged by less than poverty
> just off the O'Connell Street of our new towns

All of which poses that most crucial of all problems for the theist, why evil? A tentative solution is that, in some mysterious way, those of us who manage to survive vicariously live the lives of those who suffer and especially the lives of those most vulnerable to violence, children, such as a Down's Syndrome child or unborn children whose lives are taken from them in abortion — an original idea that is one of Egan's most profound:

> is the world which so many miss
> realized for them you'd wonder through others
> do we carry it for this mongol child that
> bucketful of abortions in the sluice room?

The poet then returns to the confession of his private needs. In contrast to the world of violence, we have the purity of nature in the sea and the rock, which, though uncompromising, 'tells no lies.' Similarly, the experience of the poet, who soundlessly cries out, is authentically human, as he watches the waves coming into the shore, and contrasts them with the scream of the tortured and the impoverished lives of the outcasts of society. This, then, is not shallow self-indulgence, but something profound, because it unites the spiritual side of puny man with the majesty of nature, with the redemptive power of the sea. And since the poet has given eloquent testimony to his awareness of political and social problems, he is perfectly entitled to ask for and expect forgiveness:

> at times I need this deep
>
> forgive me

TWO

Background

1

Desmond Egan is of Catholic stock from the south of Ireland, born on the Connacht side of Athlone in 1936. His father Tom had a varied career, owning for many years a shop selling televisions, radios, and bicycles, and, later, antiques. Athlone novelist John Broderick claimed that he saw Tom Egan, a popular bold character, as the voice of Athlone. Egan's mother Kathleen taught locally as a primary teacher in three schools in Goldsmith country for some 40 years, and taught Desmond to read at the age of 3.

Egan, therefore, belongs to a generation that grew up in the formative years of the Irish Free State and his work necessarily reflects this background. This, of course, immediately distinguishes Egan from the many poets from the North of Ireland who have come to prominence in recent times, Heaney and Montague, for example. Not only will he have a different perspective on the Northern Ireland problem itself, but Egan will deal with things in general from a distinctive viewpoint, that of the Southern Catholic at home in his state, in its majority church, its landscape — even if there are aspects of that state that he doesn't like.

Egan was educated first at primary school in Athlone town and for two years at the Marist Brothers College there. He then moved on as a boarder to the diocesan secondary school in Mullingar, St. Finian's. Here in 1950-55 Egan learnt not just English and Irish, but also Greek and Latin, and this school was obviously of major importance for his development. He writes in English, is fluent in Irish, which he loves, and regards Latin and especially Greek as very important. In the poem 'Not on the course' Egan sarcastically remarks that the glories of spring 'are like Latin and Greek which most parents agree/ought to be dropped from the Syllabus' (CP 133). He is, of course, not one of the dubious majority.

After secondary school, Egan proceeded to St. Patricks's College, Maynooth, for the years 1955-62. Here he obtained an honors B.A. in English Language and Literature, heading the class from First Arts to B.A. level; as added first year subjects, he had Greek, Latin and Logic. Egan was taught English by the late Professor Peter Connolly, a very fine critic who was a

formative influence on the poet and about whom he has written a fine essay.[1]
After leaving Maynooth, Egan first taught Greek for a couple of years at his
old school, St. Finian's in Mullingar, and then went on to University College,
Dublin. Here he took an honors Higher Diploma in Education in 1964-65.
Egan then went on to an M.A. in English, taken, unusually, by both
examination and major thesis; he achieved first-class honors, with exception-
ally high marks. Egan's supervisor was another fine critic, the late John
Jordan, and the topic of his thesis 'The Modern Irish Novel,' a work that
included comparisons with the treatment of religion in Continental authors
such as Bernanos and Mauriac.

Egan returned to St. Finian's for the period of 1965-71, where he taught both
Greek and English. In 1971 he moved to St. Patrick's Classical School in
Navan and in 1972 to Newbridge College, where he taught English until 1987.
Since then Egan has devoted himself full-time to writing.

In 1981 Egan married Vivienne Abbott, a lecturer in French at Cathal
Brugha Street College of Catering and herself the author of three books: *Menu
French Explained, Irish Cooking in Colour*, and *An Irishman's Revolution—
The Abbé Edgeworth and Louis XVI*. They have two daughters: Kate born in
1983 and Bébhinn (Irish for Vivienne) born in 1985.

2

The accidents of personal life, crucial though they may be, do not constitute
the essence of a writer, of a poet; for that one must go to his or her intellectual
and spiritual development, a development that of necessity takes place in a
particular cultural context. Within that context a crucial element for a poet is
the poetry that has immediately preceded him. In the case of contemporary
Irish poetry the two key poets that precede living artists are Yeats and
Kavanagh.

To begin with, the case of Yeats. It is beyond reasonable doubt that Yeats
is one of the greatest poets to write in English in this century, not least because
he freed himself from a 19th century idiom in middle age and went on to write
the great modern volumes *The Tower* and *The Winding Stair*. As Eliot
memorably said of Yeats, 'He was one of those few whose history is the history
of their own time, who are a part of the consciousness of an age which cannot
be understood without them.'[2] But what holds true for the critic does not
necessarily apply to the creative artist: the post-Yeatsian Irish poet can
contemplate the awesome achievement of Yeats only with misgiving, being
subject to the phenomenon called by Harold Bloom, 'the anxiety of influence.'[3]

Bloom, following Freud, believes that in the context of English Romantic poetry each successive poet strives to come to terms with and transcend his predecessors and does so by employing a series of stratagems to rewrite these predecessors. Bloom regards this anxiety as a late development and speaks of influence as *generous* during 'an age that goes all the way from Homer to Shakespeare.'[4] For the post-Yeatsian Irish poet the anxiety of influence clearly manifested itself in regard to Yeats, as this quotation from Austin Clarke establishes:

So far as the younger generation of poets are concerned . . . Yeats was rather like an enormous oak-tree which, of course, kept us in the shade . . . we always hoped that in the end we would reach the sun, but the shadow of the great oak-tree is still there.[5]

To counteract this baneful anxiety about Yeats, those poets who came after him proceeded in two inextricably linked ways: in the first place, they rendered Yeats innocuous by refusing to go down his road and trying to find a radically different road; in the second, they went on to discover a different, more amenable model, which was to make them independent of Yeats.

That model, as is well known, has often been Patrick Kavanagh. Critics, if not poets, may well feel that, if Kavanagh had not existed, it would have been necessary to invent him.[6] But Kavanagh is there and what he has done above all is to validate the ordinary experiences of life, to demonstrate that they can be transmuted into poetry: Kavanagh has made it acceptable to write of daily life on a small farm in Monaghan or on the streets of Dublin. In this he is the poetic counterpoint of Joyce.[7]

In this preoccupation with the ordinary, Kavanagh is, of course, radically different from Yeats. Yeats began his poetic career by using a highly artificial language and, even when he modernized that language in his middle and late periods, the events he describes are always stylized, ritualistic, ceremonial; it is not enough that they *exist*, they must exist *as part of ceremony*. Consider, for example, the earthy situation of a woman crying out during sexual intercourse with a man in the poem 'His Memories'; the language she uses — 'strike me if I shriek' — is very stylized, as can be seen from substituting the ordinary 'hit me if I shout.' Yeats, it seems, is incapable of allowing that the *quidditas* of anything can be just itself.

In his championing of the ordinary, Kavanagh is in the mainstream of the modern, because one of its central thematic developments, in the poetry of the 20th century, which brings it far beyond the awareness of everyday life in Hardy, is that it is willing and eager to appropriate *any and every sort of material*. There is nothing of which poetry can not be made, for in modern poetry, as Leavis points out, 'the poet assumes the right to use any materials that seem to him significant.'[8] The old Romantic reliance on traditional images of beauty has gone by the board: as Yeats caustically observed,

'Tristram and Iseult were not a more suitable theme than Paddington Railway Station.'[9] Hence in early Eliot we read of urban squalor: 'the pools that stand in drains'; 'faint stale smells of beer'; 'a morsel of rancid butter.'[10] Hence Pound in the *Cantos* has no hesitation in writing about economic history and the economic history of medieval Byzantium at that.[11] And hence Kavanagh regards the naming of everyday, prosaic things as crucial, since the poet is one who can find 'God's breath in common statement.' As he puts it in 'The Hospital':

> This is what love does to things: the Rialto Bridge,
> The main gate that was bent by a heavy lorry
> The seat at the back of a shed that was a suntrap.
> Naming these things is the love-act and its pledge;
> For we must record love's mystery without claptrap,
> Snatch out of time the passionate transitory.[12]

The daily things celebrated by Egan are many and varied: shopping in a supermarket; the poet's former house; his old car; his clothes; getting petrol.[13] The poem 'Almost February' (CP 132) provides a good example of how Egan views everyday things in practice:

> Moloney shouts a *Ho* and raises one hand
> flying by on his motorbike to work
>
> and the cry lingers
> like an image cut in light
> as the birds and hills of clouds the tractor the fullness
> take over again
>
> and even though the radio has already carried
> *The North* with a man shot dead in his bed at 4 a.m.
> slaughter in Lebanon
> the heartless Russian grab at Angola
> — so many including a few from home who didn't make this spring —
> like cold air into my cottage
>
> in spite of all that or partly because of it or whatever
> I make myself a promise once more
> to love every minute of this morning coming up like a
> snowdrop
> this day this fresh time
> simple as joy that is also old as the hills
>
> and let my shout back after the echoes

What is described here — a greeting, a response — is, at the most obvious level, extremely ordinary. But from another perspective the experience is profoundly meaningful. Set in the Midland landscape to be examined in the next chapter, the poem raises the question of the metaphysical status of our daily doings and, specifically, how they relate to the world at large. The inference to be drawn is that the events of world politics are not necessarily more important than quotidian events in our own lives and the poet is totally committed to loving the beautiful day he experiences. Consequently, the stress is on the act of mutual greeting, which contrasts with the murder and death found in a larger world. This greeting is part of a very specific early morning in January, whose *haeceitas* is stressed by the triple repetition of the demonstrative adjective 'this': at just this moment, in just this place, something good, something positive is taking place as part of everyday life and is felt to transcend the disastrous things happening elsewhere in the world.

This preoccupation with the local or parochial must be distinguished, Kavanagh firmly states, from the provincial:

Parochialism and provincialism are opposites. The provincial has no mind of his own; he does not trust what his eyes will see until he has learned what the metropolis — towards which his eyes are turned — has to say on the subject . . . The parochial mentality on the other hand is never in any doubt about the social and artistic validity of his parish. All great civilizations are based on parochialism.[14]

That is well said and the poem 'Epic' clinches the point:

> I have lived in important places, times
> When great events were decided, who owned
> That half road of rock, a no-man's land
> Surrounded by our pitch-fork armed claims.
> I heard the Duffys shouting 'Damn your soul'
> And old McCabe stripped to the waist, seen
> Step the plot defying blue cast-steel —
> 'Here is the march along these iron stones'.
> That was the year of the Munich bother. Which
> Was more important? I inclined
> To lose my faith in Ballyrush and Gortin
> Til Homer's ghost came whispering to my mind
> He said: I made the Iliad from such
> A local row. Gods make their own importance.[15]

Kavanagh, then, with his radical championing of the parochial has offered Irish poets a way out of the shadow of Yeats. In Bloom's terms we are speaking of influence that is *generous*, that causes no anxiety: Kavanagh is an enabling, a liberating force, who offers a very different road than that of Yeats and one which allows poets to develop in their own individual way. (An analogous situation existed in Latin literature where the liberating figure of Callimachus allowed Catullus, Propertius, and others to write in their own special way).[16]

So Egan is very clear about his admiration for Kavanagh:

Whereas in Yeats there is a movement towards wholeness, a striving to get to Byzantium, which is never actually achieved, in Kavanagh that wholeness is taken for granted. Out of local matters Kavanagh can, therefore, engineer a remarkable intensity that transcends its immediate origins; as he said himself, the *Iliad* came out of a local row. I find nourishment in Kavanagh that I do not find in Yeats.[17]

Indeed such is the importance of Kavanagh as a liberating force for Egan that he makes remarkable claims for Kavanagh that the critic may regard as excessive, but which are essential for the poet:

So I will conclude by laying my cards simply on the table and saying that for me, Patrick Kavanagh more and more seems the most gifted, the most important, the most necessary Irish poet of this century, bar none.[18]

There is, however, a problem with Kavanagh: his thematic range is limited. Because of this limitation, John Montague was led to comment with considerable pungency: 'Mr. Patrick Kavanagh's honesty of vision, for instance, has been liberating; but it has liberated us into ignorance: he has literally nothing to say.'[19] This overstates the case — Kavanagh celebrates the ordinary, is powerful in 'The Great Hunger,' has written some fine religious poems — but does direct our attention to his lack of a wide thematic range and his technique can consequently seem a bit dated.

And not just Kavanagh. For all its manifold achievements, Irish poetry after Yeats and Kavanagh arouses a lingering disquiet, a disquiet that it is too narrowly conceived, too restricted in topic, too ephemerally personal. Strictures that can be summed up in Aidan Matthews' dictum — where we must substitute Kavanagh's term 'provincial' for his 'parochial' — 'Our poetry is, without nuance of distaste, parochial.'[20]

The phenomenon is not, of course, confined to Ireland; as Pound wrote, 'The poverty of modern art movements lies in the paucity of mental reference of its artists.'[21] And a spectacular example is provided by English poets such as Larkin and Kingsley Amis. Amis is indeed trenchant in his exaltation of ignorance:

Nobody wants any more poems about philosophers or paintings or moralists or art galleries or mythology or foreign cities or other poems. At least I hope nobody wants them.[22]

The reductive programme implicit in this is that of extreme self-indulgence: 'I am sitting here,/I see something passing' — this is very important (I don't know why). Such banal verse is, of course, entirely predictable; as William Cookson has written, 'Much twentieth century poetry bores because it expresses the predictable.'[23]

Very few Irish poets, however, have transcended Kavanagh's limited thematic range and one of these is Desmond Egan. While Egan is very clear about his admiration for Kavanagh, as we have seen, Egan's thematic range far outstrips that of Kavanagh: he has written not just about the Irish Midlands and the town of Athlone, but also poems about the political state of Ireland, North and South; not just an elegiac sequence for his father, but also elegies for the American poets, Pound and Berryman; not just poems about shopping and getting petrol, but also poems about international politics in Chile, South Africa, the Philippines; in short, poems not only about Lough Owel, but also about Thucydides.

What we can say about Egan is that he has finally married the knowledge of Yeats with the local intensity of Kavanagh. The result is that Egan matches up to Louis MacNeice's requirements for a poet:

I would have a poet able-bodied, fond of talking, a reader of the newspapers, capable of pity and laughter, informed in economics, appreciative of women, involved in personal relationships, actively interested in politics, susceptible to physical impressions.[24]

As well as Kavanagh, there is another, and very different Irish writer who has influenced Egan, Samuel Beckett. What Beckett offers is both an avant-grade technique and a refusal to be silent in the face of the horrors of 20th century living; as Egan says, 'It simply will not do to look backwards in anger or nostalgia.'[25] He goes on to praise Beckett:

Beckett is the best we've got because he looks at the abyss, he looks at the meaningless, the chaos, the tragedy, he's aware of it in the marrow of his bones, he lives it, it's him. And in spite of that, in spite of his recognition of the awfulness of living in modern times, he still finds something to say and to live for. The thing about Beckett is that he's life-affirming. Everybody say's he's pessimistic, but he's exactly the opposite. He affirms life in the face of an extraordinary sense of meaningless, of chaos, and he still says, "I can't go on, I must go on, I go on."[26]

Or, as Egan describes him in his poem 'Echo's Bones' (SF 13-14):

> . . . our navigator our valiant necessary
> wanderer to the edges of this interpreted world

3

Ireland is, of course, not the world and Egan should be placed in the broader context of modern poetry world-wide. Here we must begin with Hugh Kenner's magisterial pronouncement at the launching of Egan's *Collected Poems* in Washington, D.C.:

> With Desmond Egan we come to a poet who is hospitable in a new way to the literary traditions of Europe and America — in a way no English poet is.

There can be no doubt that Kenner has given us a correct assessment of Egan's allegiances which range from Sophocles to Ritsos, from Machado to Lorca, from Pound to Berryman.

While Egan is himself sceptical about the concept of 'influence,' believing, rightly, that a serious poet must acquire his own unique voice, he is nevertheless indebted to the Greeks, to modern Continental writers, and to the Americans. Indeed Egan explicitly acknowledges that his first volume *Midland* owes something to Greek epigram,[27] that short, sharp, highly chiselled form that is apparently so simple and in reality so complex; as with the poems 'Thucydides and Lough Owel,' 'The Northern Ireland Question,' and 'Pike.' The whole question of Egan's Greek interests requires more detailed treatment, which it receives in Chapter Seven.

It is notoriously difficult to pinpoint 'influence,' but we can say that *the whole tone* of Egan's poetry is akin to that of modern Continental and American poetry.[28] The rhythms are those of contemporary speech, though speech that is pared down to the minimum; the language is hard and clear; the treatment direct and hard-hitting. Part of the explanation for this lies in Egan's lengthy travels in Europe and America. Indeed, like Pound and Eliot, he often makes use of the languages he has encountered. Consider, for example, the use of other languages in the collection *Snapdragon*: not only the two official languages of Ireland, Irish and English, but also in 'Morning in wind and new sounds' the words of a German song; in 'Je t'aime' the further German term *liebchen*, as well as the French and Greek for 'I love you'; in 'Why is it that your *ave atque vale*' not only the Latin of Catullus, but also the Spanish *amada mia*; and in the last poem of the sequence a French title — 'Dernier Espoir' — an epigraph from the work of Verlaine, one of Egan's favorite poets.

Of modern Continental writers, Egan feels a special kinship with the Russians and the Spanish. On record as claiming that reading Dostoievsky in translation has changed the course of his life[29] — 'he put manners on me changed me, quietened me for keeps' — Egan in the poem 'Learning Russian' (SF 23-24) is unstinting in his praise of great Russian poets such as Akhmatova whose 'words still follow me like sad eyes'; such as Mandelstam 'whose longing speaks straight to the heart' and who features in the poem 'Snow snow snow snow' (CP 198); such as early Mayakovsky who 'became a pal.' As Egan read these poets, the music of Russia became 'more nourishing than any studies' and led to the much broader ranger of themes in his later work.

Moving on to Spain, we find that Egan's first choice here is Antonio Machado, whom he esteems for his pure lyric note, his simple intensity. Also important is Lorca, favoured for his dislocation from prose statement, his imagination and the rare excitement that results. Then of Miguel Hernandez who died in 1942 during the Spanish Civil War, Egan asserts that his 'achievement and stature have not since been matched by any Spanish poet' and singles out, in particular, the poem 'Como el toro,' of which he says:

In its mixture of passion and detachment, of realist metaphor and surrealist conceit, of personal dilemma and universal application it seemed not only a fine quintessential Spanish poem but a great human drama.[30]

The other great foreign influence on Egan is American. American English as practised by Pound and Berryman has clearly influenced the tone and rhythms of Egan's poetry, has provided the devices of no capital letters for the beginning of lines, pervasive asyndeton, the subversion of line ends, a refusal to rhyme, rejection of the predictable iambic beat, as well as the capacity to use any kind of material as grist to the poetic mill. Indeed in the poem 'Pound's Castle' (CP 205-06) Egan acknowledges Pound as the doyen of the whole Modernist enterprise in English — 'Eliot Joyce Miller Lewis Cummings Bunting Yeats' — and in an interview asserts that Pound's verse 'constitutes the greatest body of poetry from the United States in this century.'[31] No wonder, then, that Egan explicitly cites Pound as an influence on his own poetry in his fine elegy 'Late but! one for Ezra' (CP 136-37): 'these few lines from my time that would have been worse/only for you.'

Another American admired by Egan is John Berryman, honored in the early poem 'For John Berryman' (CP 49-50). The poem focuses on Berryman's suicide in 1973 — Egan had written him a letter three weeks before — when he threw himself from a bridge onto the ice of the Mississippi river. Here Egan pays homage to Berryman not just by what is said, but also by *how* it is said: part of the tribute resides in the style, which is entirely apposite given Egan's beliefs that Berryman 'revitalized the sonnet form' and that he ranks next to Pound in modern American poetry.

4

So far we have talked about Egan's literary allegiances. But he himself regards music and visual art as at least equally important. Indeed Egan is on record as stating that 'If I had another existence I think it might be as a musician'; that 'Music continually runs through my head'; and that the idea for the volume *Seeing Double* may have come from painting.[32]

The music that Egan listens to every day is of three kinds: Classical, Irish traditional, and jazz. (He has no time for comtemporary pop music which he regards as 'a dead-end').[33] What serious music of these types offers the poet is the tragic sense of life, as in Beethoven's quartets, the piano concertos of Mozart, and Sibelius. Jazz is specially fruitful because of its experimental nature, its continual inventiveness and, above all, its rhythm. The rhythms of jazz musicians whom Egan likes — the saxophone players Charles Parker and Sonny Rollins, the avant-garde pianist Cecil Taylor, the trombonist Albert Mangelsdorff — permeate his poetry and, in particular, the brilliant, experimental volume *Siege!* So American influence derives not just from poets but also, and perhaps more potently, from creative jazz. In its inventiveness it shares at least one feature with traditional Irish music where the tune is never repeated in exactly the same way, nor the same tune played twice in a night.

A friend of the painter Brian Bourke and the sculptor James McKenna (one of whose poems features in the sub-text of 'Launching the book' [CP 315] and about whom Egan has written an essay), Egan regards visual art as very important and has used drawings and photographs by a number of artists to illustrate his poetry: in addition to Bourke (*Midland*) and McKenna (*Poems for Peace*), Charles Cullen (*Leaves* and *A Song For My Father*), Giacometti sculpture (*Woodcutter*), photography by Fergus Bourke (*Athlone?*) and by Liam Lyuns (*Peninsula*), painting by Alex Sadkowsky (*Seeing Double*). All this reflects the fact that Egan painted a lot as a child and is deeply interested in various periods of visual art: in Greek art, especially that of the Archaic and Hellenistic periods, the latter of which he sees as having contemporary relevence because of its 'mix of control, intuition, and chaos';[34] in the masters of Gothic and Byzantine art; in Expressionism, particularly in Lovis Corinth

25

and the German school; in contemporary art as practised by Giacometti, Francis Bacon, Rothko, Warhol, and others; and in Irish art, especially in the painting of Brian Bourke and Roderic O'Conor, and the sculpture of James McKenna, whom Egan considers the best Irish sculptor of the century.[35]

As with jazz, what Egan most values in the work of preferred modern artists is its contemporary idiom and content, expressed in an experimental way that involves the breaking of boundaries and the discovery of a new consciousness. Indeed one new form devised by Egan, that of the sub-text as seen in particular in the volumes *Seeing Double* and *A Song For My Father* derives from painting, from the portraits of Giacometti and Francis Bacon (born in Dublin) that reflect 'two different moods or responses coming out of a situation.'[36]

Furthermore, many of Egan's early imagist poems such as 'Midland' and 'Clare: The Burren' appear to offer us different views of one place, as though they were landscapes depicted by a painter.

Visual art can also become in itself the subject of a poem as with the painter Alex Sadkowsky, who is lauded as a 'blackbird of the dark sky woods', 'Kybisteter,' which deals with a Minoan Crete statuette of an acrobat vaulting a bull., and *Homenage* in which a Bourke painting figures. The artist James McKenna appears in that intense poem, 'Launching the Book'.

THREE

The Lovely Midland Sky: Landscape

1

From at least the 9th century on and to a degree greater than in any other Western country, poetry in Ireland has been notable for its sense of place. Concerned with the vivid depiction of landscape or with the moods of nature, it has continued with this preoccupation through Goldsmith in the 18th century to Yeats, Ledwidge, and Kavanagh on to the present day. Place is likely to be important to the Irish poet and so it proves in the case of Desmond Egan. While Egan has written a collection about the Dingle Peninsula in Kerry in the south-west of Ireland and about various other parts of the country, the predominant landscape in his poetry is that of the Irish Midlands, both town and country. This is the area of the central lowlands, marked by no hills of any great size; raised peat bogs which can reach depths of up to 10 metres in some locations; an elaborate system of rivers and lakes and indeed canals; a wide variety of cloud formations; and a large number of small market towns.[1]

Egan sets out to record the everyday life of the Irish Midlands, an area he loves and one far removed from Donough MacDonagh's derogatory 'soft and dreary midlands.'[2] Two of Egan's volumes in particular focus upon the Midlands. His first, *Midland*, is mainly concerned with the rural landscape; and his fifth, *Athlone?*, with the town of that name. Egan there does for the Midlands what Yeats did for Sligo, Joyce for Dublin, and Kavanagh for Monaghan. As Kavanagh said about the things of rural life in Monaghan:

I name their several names

Until a world comes to life —
Mornings, the silent bog,
And the God of imagination waking

27

To record the essence of a place for posterity is no easy task and Egan asserts of the Midlands that 'I had to discover it, nearly invent it.'[4] Because the Midlands are not just a place, a landscape — though they are certainly that — but also a state of mind, a *Weltanschauung*. Egan's poem 'At the Birthplace of Oliver Goldsmith' (SF 41-44) makes this clear, when he evokes Goldsmith the man:

> — more of a peasant's look or maybe I should say
> *a country fella's* (my father's category)
> rooted and physical — well *midland*
> not without that hint of the complacent we
> still have to guard against
>
> yes and I think we'd hear even in your quick talk
> our very drawl in which there are no mountains only
> rivers of raincloud slowing along
> through low fields where the cattle graze but
> ready like yours to laugh

2

That Egan publishes books rather than poems is readily seen in the volumes *Midland* and *Athlone?*: both volumes concentrate upon the Irish Midlands, and both begin and end with programmatic poems. Already in the opening poem 'Midland' of Egan's first volume *Midland* (CP 19), we observe the truth of Connolly's dictum that 'This relatively plain and colorless imagery is more radically transforming than anything in Ledwidge or Kavanagh';[5] that this typically Midland landscape of bog, clouds, crows is peopled; that it is presented in concentrated imagist style that suggests 'a scene captured on canvas';[6] and that in phrases such as 'horizon afternoon,'[7] 'flat as drainwater,' and the lack of capital letters and of punctuation the poem reveals its resolutely modernist approach:

> a house steamed down the horizon afternoon
> the bog sea calm
> flat as drainwater the swells of brown rising
> to where quiet mountains of cloud sheered ranging away
> like another dimension
>
> and gulls wandered searching in space for their souls

Although the volume *Midland* deals with an introspective figure in the *Midlands*, its closing programmatic poem, 'Dialogue' (CP 58), envisages this figure living there with another person, the house of the poem 'Midland' becoming a stone cottage. But this indeed is no sooner presented than it is abandoned by the poet speaking, unlike Yeats in 'Inisfree,' as a realist and with wry humour; the ideal retreat is not available to the birds, still less to humans:

> *there is very little I want really —*
> *a stone cottage on the edge of a lake*
> *darkened with woods*
> *(there would have to be woods)*
> *and of course some someone special*
> *we could live there quietly with the birds*
>
> you don't want much my friend
> just more than anyone has ever managed
>
> even the birds

In approximately half the poems that are sandwiched in *Midland* between these two programmatic poems, Egan proceeds to chronicle, to name the names, of what makes the Irish Midlands 'Midland': the birds such as gulls, crows, larks, swans, wild duck; coarse fish such as perch and pike; animals such as foxes, squirrels, and horses; flowers and fauna such as dahlias, crocus, yews, furze, fern, nettles; water in the form of rivers, lakes, canals; even place names such as Owel, Boyne, Heronstown. As a consequence, the landscape of the Midlands is metamorphosed through the power of language, so that it becomes for us a new creation, a new world that has its own special and unique atmosphere.

In chronicling this other world, Egan not only deals with conventional topics such as the passing of summer ('September' — CP 21) or cycle of a flower like its crocus ('Crocus a white crocus' — CP 53-55) for his own purposes; he is also prepared to take on Midland topics that may seem unpoetic, even anti-poetic such as pike, perch, nettles, a canal. A fine example of Egan's early imagism, the poem 'Pike' (CP 43), which consists of a mere 15 words in 5 lines (the last two of which have only one word), captures with delicate conciseness a traumatic moment in the life of the fish in one of these 'reedy rivers that wander through fertile loam'[8] and establishes a rapport between fish and poet, between landscape and man:

doubt-sensitive eyer your mad fright
across shallows of reedy sunlight   towards
the drop

frightens
me

The rapport that is implicit in 'Pike' becomes explicit in 'Perch' (CP 33), 'a common spiny-finned freshwater fish (*perca fluviatilis*).'[9] The poet first astringently refutes the received opinion that the perch is of no value and empathizes with its often unpleasant fate:

common and worthless *in the common opinion*
they skit in gangs dumpy flashing their ink-red
for the baits of only-youngsters
to be secretly tossed bent now gaping
out to the dog (as often as not?)
electrocuted netted dumped in shovelfuls
to make room for any trout . . . poor perch

In contrast to 'the common opinion' he then offers his own very positive evaluation of the perch, his *laudes percae*, stressing its speed in the water or capacity to remain still; its identification with a nice day and precious moments in the summer; its beauty:

as if they can't
                zip the passing waters
                                wordswift

or swing like silver bangles down a river

halfrise
on some circled   lazily circling   pond and
say a young day

— or maybe stand pulsing in a chest of weeds: the heartbeat
of a retired canal

many a boy
jerks (over the bikes and daisies) his first catch
and finds himself gaping at
                                more than a perch there
twisting in his hands

oh vowels of summers!

It is impossible to imagine a poem entitled 'Nettles' (CP 24) by any of the English Romantic poets who write about landscape, up to and including Yeats. But Egan, against the odds, contrives such a poem, a veritable *culpae urticae*.[10] As in the poems about pike and perch, there is a connection between nettles, which are personified, and the human, but here that connection is negative rather than positive; the rich green and fruitfulness of the nettle cannot hide its uselessness, its malevolence, so that it takes on a deeper symbolic meaning identified not merely with the physical waste-land of death and destruction, but also with a metaphysical one:

> decadent harvest ripening emerald
> in silences of moon and the night you
> thrum with acid power just to produce
> that wrinkly toppling crop
> sting-fruited fanatically baited
> in treacherous luxuriance
> waving the bite of each touch
> only to guard your nothing
>
> green rash!   growth
> of graveyards dumps and every wilderness
> I have seen you sunless one
> spread elsewhere spread
> down the waste places of the soul

This refusal to be sentimental about nature is found also in the brief, but powerful poem 'Near Herons Town March 19th' (CP 25):

> one lark escaping up
> above hills that huddled
> like the crowd after mass
>
> no river — only furze
> bursting crocus round a thornbush
> where brown sacks: two fox cubs
> minus tails had been hung
> updown
> still grinning through their teeth

From the title, which establishes place and date, onwards, the poem is incredibly specific — one lark, no river, two fox cubs — and this specificity is employed to offer a negative assessment of the landscape, even crocus being linked to a thornbush (lines 1-5). Then the concluding, very vivid image (lines 6-9), in which specificity is maintained, teaches us that foxes, though part of the landscape, are regarded here only as vermin, that there is a price on their heads or, rather, their tails, cut off for the bounty, and, finally, and paradoxically, even in death the young foxes — there are two as opposed to the solitary lark — retain their animal nature and indeed their wild beauty. A poem, then, that combines exemplary clarity with total honesty — both qualities we associate with the Greeks.

The artificial waterway, which links the mighty river Shannon in the town of Athlone and which is the subject of the poem 'Canal' (CP 29), is not merely animate, not merely attuned to human beings as in the pathetic fallacy, but is treated as an actual person — note the 7 occurrences of the personal pronoun 'you' and 4 of the possessive adjective 'your' — who plays an important part in the life of the community. What Egan does here is to reverse the usual way we look at an entity such as a canal: instead of our doing things to it, it, or rather he, reacts to us; a point emphasized by the fact that the Station and Barracks of the town are also personified. Athlone is therefore alive not only with its people, but with everything in it. So this canal can talk, has a Midland drawl, goes for a stroll, salutes people:

> a drawling shake-hands and you stroll from the river
> — how often we watched your watery serge
> walking the terrace in the quiet of Gentex
> and wandering slowly down the Batteries
> saluting everyone

It should not be thought, however, that Egan's Midlands lack real people. We find there not only the poet as ubiquitous observer, but also other people such as the tennis players of 'Drops' (CP 28), those attending a burial in 'I stood with her brother' (CP 23), a sick women in 'Memory of Kate' (CP 51), and another woman and a petrol attendant in 'Filling Up' (CP 26).

Of these, the poem 'Filling Up' offers the most sustained treatment of the human theme. The place is again the town of Athlone, the event, stressed by the ring composition of first and last lines, the buying of petrol on a Sunday for the poet's car; a very ordinary occurrence, which suddenly takes on deeper meanings. One reason is that for the theist *everything* has a unique value because it mirrors the transcendent world — note the appearance of God in line 5; another is that when people are involved, each of them, as the poem 'Unique' (CP 202) has taught us, is surprisingly unique. Immediately after the opening line establishes that petrol is gushing into the tank *unseen*, the poet *sees* across the street a woman who is identified by her clothes, just as the poet is in 'Unique,' and by her car, as the poet is in 'Goodbye old Fiat' (CP 187-88). He thinks he recognizes this woman who is named Kathleen and so identified with Ireland (Kathleen Ni Houlihan); she is symbolic, that is, of many Irish mothers out for a drive on Sunday with a car full of children, while father is in the pub or at a match:

> . . . petrol rising unseen
>   I can see
> boots across from the Royal Hotel,
> sheepskin coat a darker head
> (God! it could be Kathleen) bending
> to the lock of a dinged Cortina

Meanwhile, the car has been filled with petrol and he is ready to drive off. The words exchanged between him and the petrol attendant are basic, part of the ritual, but the poet rejects the offer of stamps and the commercialism they imply. Unlike the woman, he is leaving that kind of world behind, heading elsewhere, off on an adventure. Consequently, the petrol, though still unseen, is now personified, singing with joy:

> unseen the petrol sings

3

One of Egan's most homogeneous volumes, *Athlone?* consists of 22 poems which are all about the Midland town. Situated almost exactly in the center of Ireland, Athlone is a thriving market town characterized by narrow streets (one of which is captured in Fergus Bourke's photograph at the beginning of the volume); by a large variety of small shops and pubs; by that intimate atmosphere which small towns possess (and which has been well caught by the distinguished Athlone novelist John Broderick); by a peculiar use of the English language, modified even today by certain Elizabethan pronunciations and Gaelic idioms; by the river Shannon, which divides Ireland into West and East; and by the canal we have already encountered.

With the poet more overtly present than in Midland, *Athlone?* lovingly chronicles the life of Egan's home town: people such as shopkeepers, undertakers, barbers; places like the Mill, the library, the Ritz cinema; streets such as Egan's Connaught Street, O'Connell Street, Pipe Lane, Bastion Street, Asicus Villas; neighboring areas such as the cemetery at Cornamagh, Clonown, Hodson Bay, Baylough, the famous Clonmacnois; typically Midland names such as Egan, Derwin, McCormack, as well as other Irish names such as Halligan, Henry, Moylan, Connaugton, McCracken, McNeill, O'Meara, Logan, Ward; and, interwoven into all of this, events in the poet's life such as finishing at the Convent school, going to boarding school, buying sweets, reading comics, cycling round the town, illicitly smoking, bringing back books to the library, leaving Athlone.

In all of this Egan effectively captures the atmosphere of Athlone, so that the town becomes for us a living thing; as Conor Johnston has written, 'One of the major successes in this volume lies in the manner in which Egan brings to life his boyhood responses to the town-world around him.'[11]

The opening programmatic poem of *Athlone?* which is itself called 'Athlone?' immediately presents us with a problem: given that the entire volume is devoted to the minute particulars of the Midland town, why the question mark? Egan has suggested the answer in an interview:

I know that town, not as well as my father, but I know it . . . Yet who knows all about any place? To take on, to try to represent the complexity of a small town and to make large statements about it to me would seem arrogant. Everyone discovers some facet of a place, and nobody discovers all of it . . . The question mark has a little touch of humor in it, because midlanders don't claim to be all that sure about anything, even about whether the ground will open in front of your feet ten yards down the road.[12]

Nevertheless, as detail follows detail, the doubt expressed in the question mark is well and truly alleviated 21 poems later! Indeed the very first and typographically separate line of the poem 'Athlone?' equates the town with nothing less than the Garden of Eden before and after the Fall, with, that is, the totality of the human condition in its state both of primeval grace and later corruption, so that Athlone becomes a microcosm of both the transcendent and material worlds. Consequently, Athlone — like the Midlands in general — is not merely a place, though with its characteristically narrow streets it is certainly that, but also a distinctive and ubiquitous mode of being, *une manière d'être*, in which people and landscape complement each other and which manifests itself in a local accent that transcends physical utterance to become metaphysical:

> as from a garden of original sin and grace something
>
> of twisty lanes of oblique streets
> of voices calm as the landscape
> a walk a spiritual accent
> lingers in fingerprints everywhere

Conscious then that this account of a small town may seem pretentious, Egan becomes ironically self-depreciatory:

> makes me persist an interviewer of sorts
> dogged with simple questions my earphones squeaking
> *cop yourself on* because all art
> contains an element of the ridiculous

Due regard paid to this objection, Egan carries on with his efforts to define Athlone: it requires both body and soul — a soul not puffed up with egoism, but humble — to define the physical aspects of this place and the people who live in it, and these parochial things are so crucial, so powerful, that they affect us not only, as is obvious, after we are born, but also when we are in the womb, and it is they rather than the state of the kosmos at our birth who rule us:

> still
> elbows on the shiny stone my soul without ambition
> keeps trying to open a door or a street or two
> the light the footsteps the brief voices
> that pull at our amniotic fluids that fix our horoscopes
> more than any stars

The poem then modulates into its long concluding passage, itself measured like the measured pace of both the river Shannon and the lives of the people: comparing himself to a crow, a bird later called (with a wry Midland glance at Keats) the 'nightingale of our town,' that is, a singer of its praises (CP 147), the poet proceeds inexorably through the streets of Athlone with their shops, pubs, and people, all of whom and of which have a common *Weltanschauung*, towards his own home in Connaught Street, not only a real *nostos* with its attendant mixture of delight and sadness, but also an annunciation of Athlone, the poet's own unique place. The poem ends not with a place, but with a person, a person who is friendly and who, like the poet, is firmly rooted in Athlone; in fact his father, the spirit of the town, who is one of its main subjects of the volume *A Song For My Father* nine years later:

> and while the town that is only my town flows
> by with its river rhythms
> shimmery so slow and dignified with lives I
>
> will glide like a crow up the narrow causal ways
> up through shopdoors and windows the many storeys
> of an idea shared like a zodiac
> by faces that turn like gables
> by friends by neighbors
> by singsongs from pubs curling out in smoke
> uphill towards my own home
>
> bred born and reared inside me it tolls

more slowly now turning all into afternoons
with something of that sad echo of the Barrack chimes bringing
together in quiet as if everything were waiting
the sweetshops people roads the Battery hills of the past
my Connaught Street

angelus of the small place we discover
has left us in exile everywhere else

someone waves from the front door and turns back in

'Athlone?' must surely rank among the best poems written by Desmond
Egan.

The 20 poems that follow 'Athlone?' fully flesh out the ins and outs of the
town with a masterly preciseness. As promised in 'Athlone?' original sin and
original grace are both present. On the one hand, we have death (Mrs. Ned,
the undertaker); floods; the burden of history ('Williamite time,' 'British officers,' '*their* castle'); the Mill like 'a silent Platonic cave mysterious with
water'; unread books; Mrs. Healion frowning. On the other hand, the accu-
mulation of detail, of what Egan calls 'the eternally significant' (SF 44),
entitles him to make large claims for his home town: if Kavanagh lived in
important places, Egan asserts that 'I am a citizen of no mean country' (CP
160); if Kavanagh found the Grand Canal redemptive, Egan finds that daily
life can be a 'ritual' (CP 161), a 'liturgy of our own' (CP 163), and one that
takes place in 'the metaphysical street' (SF 52); and if Kavanagh thought the
parochial at least as important as world events,[13] so too does Egan's barber:

in his surgeon's coat the barber cheerily
circled the subject the way his talk did soccer
the Bomber the lads the Bomber Jackie leaving
disasters Stalin Korea unnoticed as traffic

Athlone, then, is certainly important. But this microcosm of the world
cannot last forever: Egan leaves Athlone, just as the volume of poetry comes
to an end, and so the final programmatic poem (anticipated by the immediately preceding one 'Leaving') is entitled 'Envoi,' the poet's final address to
the town and to his earlier life there.

In the 21 poems preceding 'Envoi,' Egan has filled in a great deal of very
specific physical detail about Athlone, but such is his familiarity with the
area that he is able *mentally* to envisage the local landscape, characterized
by bogs and beauty spots along the river Shannon. This he proceeds to do,
not without an awareness that dwelling on these attractions may be exces-

sive, because, as Eliot puts it, 'human kind/Cannot bear very much reality':[14]

> saying goodbye for the umpteenth time the
> mind like a pensioner drifts on a favorite walk
> up the living road towards the bogs
> that flood and colours everywhere
>
> no doubt it could catch
> this side of the tidiness of Curnabull those
> obvious moments along the Shannon
> but that's a bit much just now
> there being so little one can cope with

So he settles for a less ambitious itinerary, a less obviously attractive part of the river. In this less demanding return, as the poet imagines the Irish Midlands round Athlone, past and present, we encounter a typical mixture of sadness and happiness:

> so I go up and up the same way in hope
> as far as the cross river
> lean over the bridge and
> join the weeds the ancient shadowing of water
>
> somewhere out there
> like a hint of smoke on the breeze Clonmacnois
> rises in thought a graveyard wide with unheard goodbyes
> the skygoats are whinnying high
> high in a summer evening
> cutting sad happy celtic circles over our heads

But this ambivalence does not last. In the final analysis, Egan is positive about his area: nature is beneficent, there is a relaxed and intimate rapport between father and son ('Envoi' ending, like 'Athlone?,' with a person), landscape and people complement each other. We end with the world of the 'lovely Midland sky' (CP 192) and with two of the most evocative and beautiful lines Egan has ever written:

> the hedges have greened I am walking very slowly
> listening to my father

FOUR

I Sat Down and Wept: Elegy

1

Beginning with Callinos of Ephesus in the early 7th century B.C. the genre elegy — which comes from *elegos*, meaning 'a song of mourning' — was used in Greece for a variety of themes, one of which was the commemoration of the dead. In the Hellenistic period elegy dealing with a dead person was given a pastoral setting by Theocritus ('Lament for Daphnis'), Bion ('Lament for Adonis,' one of Shelley's models for 'Adonais'), and an unknown disciple of Bion ('Lament for Bion').

Elegy in English literature has, since the 16th century, come to mean either a contemplation of the tragic aspects of life (as in Gray's 'Elegy') or, more often, a poem of lamentation, usually written about the death of a single person. Many of these elegies are pastoral, as in Milton's 'Lycidas,' Shelley's 'Adonais,' and Arnold's 'Thyrsis,' and the pastoral setting continues in Anglo-Irish literature as late as Yeats ('Shepherd and Goatherd') and Kinsella ('A Country Walk'). But Tennyson's 'In Memoriam' abandons the pastoral setting and Yeats' 'In Memory of Eva Gore-Booth and Con Markiewicz' qualifies his praise of the dead to a degree unheard of up to that time.[1]

Chénier says 'Mais la tendre élégie et sa grâce touchante/M'ont séduit,[2] and elegy is a genre of which Egan is fond and at which he excels. While his concern with landscape allows Egan to keep the pastoral setting in poems such as 'Eugene Watters is Dead' (CP 207-8) and 'In Francis Ledwidge's Cottage' (CP 210-12), his elegies are nevertheless extremely modern in their treatment of the eternal everyday of unpretentious people like Mrs. Ned (CP 156) and the poet's father (SF 49-61); of the idiosyncrasies of a friend such as Eugene Watters (Eoghan O'Tuairisc); of the politics of modern Anglo-Irish poetry in the poem about Ledwidge; of the achievements and failings of admired poets like Berryman (SP 49-50) and Pound (CP 136-37); of the horrific realities of South Africa ('For Benjamin Moloise,' PP 13-14, SF 16-17) and of the Philippines ('For Father Romano on His 45th Birthday,' PP 23-24, SF 32-33).[3] At the same time, Egan espouses the two modes in which modern poets write elegies: they either embrace the traditional motifs of transcendence and consolation, or they resolutely refuse these and stoically face the loss and the sadness.

2

Located in the heart of the collection *Athlone?*, the poem 'Mrs. Ned' (CP 156) deals, like the rest of the poems in that volume, with the daily life of an ordinary person in a small Midland town. People like Mrs. Ned, who were not famous — like Berryman or Pound — make their apparently humdrum existence something special and precious. So in the first section of the poem, homage is paid to Mrs. Ned's daily routine as she serves in her shop, to the minute particularity of her shopcoat, slippers, bandaged leg. But there are extra special moments too and in the second section of the poem she is seen preparing for the annual Corpus Christi procession with images of faith and hope which serve to make her death more poignant and contrast with the lengthy mourning of the poet's mother:

> every year she'd have their shop window in flowers
> with candles and a Sacred Heart for the procession
> and my mother cried a long time
> the evening Mrs. Ned died

In an earlier poem 'I stood with her brother' (CP 23) the setting is a graveyard in another Midland town, Mullingar, where a young girl is being buried:

> yews hung like teardrops
> and a pigeon was brooding
> when I stood with her brother
> at the clayey tumor of
> her grave
> our few words
> being tossed by the wind
> shouted down
> by her silence

In the manner of a Greek epitaph, this poem offers no consolation, but fixes on the detail of the graveyard scene. From the first word of the poem's tightly organized single sentence, the controlling image is of nature that is threatening and ominous. Here Egan manipulates the traditional use of the pathetic fallacy in elegy, so that the yew trees, which are so often found in cemeteries and whose 'roots are wrapt about the bones,'[4] are linked to human grief in a negative way, as is the pigeon which broods like the mourners. The visually precise phrase 'clayey tumor' reminds up of our mortality — 'remember man that thou are dust and into dust thou shalt return' — and hints at the fact that the girl died of a brain tumor. Furthermore, the wind for which graveyards are notorious ensures that the conversation of the poet with the girl's brother, ironically designated by the cliché a 'few words' that is used on these occasions, is lost. But ultimately it is not, of course, nature that is the enemy, but death, and it is the enforced silence of the dead girl that renders the mourners' words totally ineffectual and is seen to do so through the vivid paradox that ends the poem, 'shouted down/by her silence.'

The poem 'Twenty Years' (CP 201) is an elegy for a friend who died in 1979. Revisiting Arklow in Co. Wicklow where he and Harkin once on a choir outing skimmed stones across the sea, the poet is initially surprised to find that things are still the same. But the sub-text from the choir's song *Now Is The Hour* undercuts all that, because it is asserting *we must say goodbye*, with the result that things are no longer the same at all:

> and foolishly now I picked another
> but not this time to skim across the
> strange unconscious surface   *soon we'll*
>   *be*
> it lies smooth as seagreen surrounded by   *sailing*
> the cards and jetsam on our mantel
> and Bobby when I look at it   *far across*
> our choirbus again parks itself sideways   *the sea*
> the stones rattle under our feet

The stone has become a reminder of days irrevocably gone, of the fact that the choir the poet and Harkin belonged to is now singing of parting, that the parting is Harkin's death, since he is '*sailing/far across/the sea.*' This death is treated in a complex series of contrasts: on the one hand, in the main text the reality of death seems somehow not to belong to Harkin, but the sub-text indicates that he is dying and wishes to be remembered, a wish already granted in the poem ('yes I remembered'); on the other hand, in the main text the detail of the room where Harkin lies in bed points to preparation for the finality of death, but the sub-text with its unfinished phrase *when I* suggests the idea that there is in fact something beyond. Thus the interaction of main and sub-text subtly catches the complex emotions engendered by the deaths of this friend who became a priest ('breviary') and who ended his life working for and among ordinary people, in an estate.

3

Egan has written a very successful series of elegies on fellow-artists, which emphasizes that his literary allegiance is both local and cosmopolitan: poems on Irish poets Ledwidge and Watters, on traditional Irish musician Kieran Collins, and on American poets Pound and Berryman.

Many consider the Pound elegy outstanding among these, but arguably the richest and most skilful elegy is the remarkable 'Eugene Watters is dead' (CP 207-08), a poem composed for the writer known in Irish as Eoghan O'Tuairisc, a distinguished novelist, dramatist and poet,[5] whose *Aifreann na Marbh* has been described by Alan Titley as 'by far the most evocative, complex and intelligently sustained lyrical achievement in modern Irish poetry.'[6] But although quotations from two of Watters' poems in English are used in the text, it is as the poet's friend rather than as a writer that he appears here.

To begin with, the poem establishes the shocking fact that Watters, who was 'unique and valiant like daylight' and who consequently 'seemed to have no truck with death,' has in fact died in 1982 at the age of 58. The unexpected nature of his death is stressed by the phrase 'the new life,' quoted in the sub-text from Watters' own wedding poem from 1972. This same emphatic juxtaposition of life and death is further emphasized by the fact that Watters' wedding and funeral Mass both took place in the Church of St. Michael's in Ballinasloe. The life lived by both Watters and and poet, who was best man at this (second) wedding in 1972 is non-materialistic, Watters being 'crazily generous innocent of bourgie values' and the poet having no coin in his pocket at the wedding; Watter's small coin, offered instead, is ironically designated by a phrase from the wedding ceremony: 'and he laid a shilling on the tray *my wordly goods.*'

The second part of the poem reflects on the significance of Watters' death and does so partly through literalizing the pastoral conventions. Here the traditional theme of flowers strewn on the bier is made literal in the emphasis on the facts that the name of Watters' wife, Margaret, comes from the Greek word for daisy, that Watters' rowboat is 'taxiing through drifts of elodia,' and that 'cyclamen and gladioli linger' in the river Barrow beside which he lived (a theme anticipated earlier in the sub-text by Watters' own reference to '*a leaf/from the/bride's bouquet*').

Adapting another pastoral motif, that of death by water, to the literal circumstances of Watters' life — he lived in a lockhouse by the Barrow — Egan employs the theme of water in two ways. Firstly, as in *Odes* of Horace such as 4.7, the eternal processes of nature, as represented by the weir beside which Watters lived (and also by the beautiful rose in Watters' poem 'The

Weekend of Dermot and Grace') point up the all too time-bound life of human beings:

> the smell of water a moon barely shivering
> that wide weir mildly continually on the ear
> o wine moments never to come again
> when hope unlatched the door and took a stool with us
> on the flags before an open fire climbed later
> up flashlamp stairs to the books a table he carpentered
> a cupboard of manuscripts but what are words
> without the speaker's *blas*
> *And a white rose by a wall in Drumcondra*
> *Is simply a shattering thing*

Secondly, as in pastoral elegy such as Theocritus' 'Lament for Daphnis,' eternal nature, through the pathetic fallacy, expresses grief at human death, grief which mirrors that of the poet, who, through the echo of *Psalm 137*, puts himself in the tradition of great human lamentation:

> the weir still breaks in quietness it says *Eugene*
> and by the lockhouse of Maganey I sat down and wept
> having thought you just as immortal

These asseverations are not left unqualified. Two rhetorical questions move us away from them. The first comes just before the passage last quoted and calls into question the reality of Watters' death:

> is it really true
> that you will not lead us across the plank the *flash* on
> down the towpath by your reedy mysterious river ever
> again?

The lines with the pathetic fallacy appear to answer the question with the assertion 'yet, it is really true,' but then the answer to the second rhetorical question, which concludes the poem — 'I was wrong was I?' — is inconclusive, 'yes and no,' the ambiguity cleverly underlined by the fact that this sentence reads the same forwards and backwards. That is, yes Watters is dead and in one sense you will never see him again, and no, although he is dead he remains alive permanently in memory, in his own writing, and in this writing about him.

Egan's elegy for the Irish poet Ledwidge — 'In Francis Ledwidge's Cottage' (CP 210-12) — which enters the politics of modern Anglo-Irish poetry with *éclat*, is likely to be regarded as the most controversial of his compositions in this genre. The poem begins by legitimately stressing Ledwidge's achievement as a nature poet, a message underlined by the sub-text, consisting of Ledwidge's poem 'Behind the Closed Eye' which embodies his characteristic delight and lucid perception of nature. Egan adds further that Ledwidge was poor and that he believed he was fighting for civilization in the First World War.

But the post-Yeatsian Irish poet who champions Ledwidge and Kavanagh is faced, inevitably, with the towering figure of Yeats. So embedded in Egan's eulogy of Ledwidge is an attack on Yeats' politics, followed by a frontal onslaught on Yeats' poetry, which is so radical that it demands a much more intense and thorough assessment of Ledwidge.

The attack on Yeats, then, is twofold: political and literary, the former much less contentious than the latter. In political terms Yeats is identified with the Anglo-Irish gentry; he was in fact middle class, but certainly came to champion the gentry, as exemplified, in particular, by Lady Gregory, and in his later years identified himself strongly with the great Anglo-Irish figures of Georgian Ireland such as Swift and Burke, out of whom he created a powerful myth. This may all be regarded as legitimate for Yeats without denying that it could also be extremely problematic for a poor Irish Catholic. Similarly, for an Irish Catholic nationalist Yeats's vacillation about the 1916 Rising in his poem 'Easter 1916' and, in particular, the line 'Was it needless death after all?' must seem unnecessarily cautious — though it must be said that Yeat's political position was, fundamentally, that of an Irish nationalist. So the complexities of Irish politics allow Egan to champion Ledwidge in that area.

But Egan proceeds then to make a breathtaking and inevitably controversial statement in which he prefers the best of Ledwidge to Yeats:

> so coming if I may to myself I prefer
> your best poems to Yeats's which over the years have
> begun to collapse on me like a mansion into words
>
> but since life has a way of shaking the academic walls
> it is your fragile truths which survive like a fanlight

Allowing for the fact that this is offered as a personal preference and not as a critical judgement; allowing that we are talking about the *best* of Ledwidge's poems and that these are indeed very fine; allowing, finally, that Egan, like all post-Yeatsian Irish poets, must develop defence mechanisms of the ego to cope with Yeats and that, in terms of poetry, the mechanisms often come down to Kavanagh and Ledwidge; allowing all that, the judgement presented here must seem, from the point of view of the critic, unacceptable. But Egan is, of course, a poet, a poet who needs to find models in the immediate past that offer liberation for his own work; and Ledwidge is clearly one such model.

But Egan has another and ultimately more valid reason for preferring Ledwidge to Yeats: Ledwidge may be regarded as depicting wholeness in a way that Yeats, torn between self and soul, swordsman and saint, could not. As a result, Ledwidge's language can seem 'the pure lyric of the only truth we want.' Even here there is a point of contact between the two Irish poets, that of Platonism, which is vital in Yeats' poetry[7] — especially in 'Under Ben Bulben' — and which Egan, referring to Plato's view that this world is like a cave, finds also in Ledwidge:

> you found
> the cave
> where language can echo reecho shadowing the only real

The preoccupation with the genre of elegy found in Egan's *Collected Poems* continues in the 1989 volume *A Song For My Father*: he has not only written an elegy for his father consisting of a sequence of 18 poems (see next section), but also elegies on the political figures Benjamin Moloise and Fr. Romano (see Chapter Six), and on the Irish musician Kieran Collins. The latter draws attention to the imporatnce of music and, in particular, traditional Irish music in Egan's life.

The elegy for Kieran Collins (SF 26-27) finds Egan at his most inconsolable and this lack of consolation is stressed all the more because Collins is regarded as unique in his playing, is identified with 'The Skylark,' a tune he had made his own, conceived of as embodying in his 'spirit notes' something quintessentially and indigenously Irish. All this musical activity 'has been interrupted for keeps' and Collins will 'never play again.' As a consequence, even though Collins' music and life have became united as one, the inconsolable poet no longer wishes to hear him and echoes Catullus' words at his brother's grave — *atque in perpetuum, frater, ave atque vale*[8] — as he says a final farewell:

> put away the whistle I don't want to hear
> in death forever my brother I'm saying goodbye

It is a measure of how the elegy today can be totally honest about its subject that Egan's poem 'For John Berryman' (CP 49-50) can focus on the moment of the great American poet's suicide in 1972, when he threw himself from a bridge onto the ice of the Mississippi river. Written in 1972 in Egan's early imagist style, the poem begins by painting the scene with a few quick strokes which emphasize both the pathos of what is happening — Berryman takes off his glasses before jumping[9] — and the character of the man — his eyes are bleary and 'amused,' as in photographs. But if the mechanics of suicide are, at one level, simple, at another they are complex, involving both pain 'throbbing like a stripped nerve' and the surrender of Berryman's achievement and promise. The appropriate response is grief.

Because Berryman, a lapsed Catholic, had come back to the Church towards the end of his life, Egan with astonishing audacity compares his last breath to the Annunciation by the archangel Gabriel to Mary, so that Berryman's death takes on paradoxically, a kind of transcendence. The key to which paradox is provided by the poem's epigraph from the *Tao*: 'Because I love so much I lose so much.' There is also a strong suggestion that Christ — whose incarnation Gabriel was announcing — will have saved and forgiven the tormented poet.

Then, as Berryman actually dies, the tone changes again and we remember that Christ, who was fully man, experienced the Crucifixion: 'Christ — who knew the fall the jerk — save us all.' So Christianity, because of the Incarnation, provides consolation of a sort. But at the same time, the poet, invoking his own understanding of what Berryman called 'the epistemology of loss,' discovers he must make use of the drug with which we all try to come to terms with death — forgetfulness in the shape of a quick whiskey — bitter like the event — a newspaper, the distraction of television. The poem, written in retrospect, can still note what is being avoided: the fact that Berryman's reign as a poet is, unlike Christ's, over. And yet, Berryman's eyes in death confront 'the lighted the innocent skies' that offer hope of salvation.

Written in his later discursive style, Egan's elegy for Pound — 'Late But! One for Ezra' (CP 136-37) — derives much of its undoubted force from reversing one of elegy's most persistent themes, that of preserving something even in death. For the poem resolutely refuses to offer Pound consolation in a variety of situations the American poet has found himself in: 'there is nothing anyone can do.' In addition, Pound's limitations are not glossed over — as a modern elegy demands.

Pound's situation was, of course, tragic. With hindsight we can see that he was foolish to back Italian Fascism (Yeats avoided that), but did so in the mistaken belief that Fascism would support his view that the international economic system was corrupt (it still is) and that the banks in particular were responsible for destroying society through usury (cf. Egan's poem 'Breaking,' CP 214). Pound broadcast from Rome on behalf of Fascism during the war and escaped execution for treason against America only at the enormous cost of spending twelve years in a psychiatric hospital in Washington, D.C., a place of pain grotesquely named after St. Elizabeth (who, when old, produced a child and is therefore someone who enhances life). When Pound was eventually released in 1957, the great poet was callously labelled in the official document of release as 'incurably insane but harmless' — a detail adverted to in Egan's poem.

This 'lunatic' was not only a major poet in his own right — Egan regards the Pisan Cantos as 'among the great achievements in poetry of our century'[10] — but also a seminal influence on the whole development of modern poetry and prose, on Yeats and Eliot, on Joyce and Lewis. The editor of 'The Waste Land,' acknowledged by Eliot as the superior craftsman, was the same man who was incarcerated in the wire cage at Pisa after the war and a man who eventually lapsed into almost total silence, about which the poet can do nothing:

> my hands are tied by time's red tape there is really nothing I can do
> to try to dissuade you *il miglior fabbro* as I dearly would
>
> from lapsing into the wire cage of silence

Nor, as a gesture of solidarity, can Egan even attend Pound's last poetry reading in Spoleto when he read Marianne Moore's poem 'What Are Years?' but none of his own.

Despite this stress on what he can not do, Egan's poem has already succeeded in doing what it claims to be unable to do, in explicitly putting on record Pound's role as a poet and as a catalytic influence on Modernism. The poem then not only pays tribute again to his tireless efforts on behalf of others, but also confronts head-on Pound's notorious anti-Semitism — he told the Jewish poet Allen Ginsberg 'But the worst mistake I made was that stupid, suburban prejudice of anti-Semitism'[11] — and places it firmly in context, unwise but part of Pound's obsession with economic justice:

> unless maybe put it on the record that even what is Jewish in us all
> forgives with a wave of the hand one who was years too sensitive
> a continent too brave and never for yourself
> so that your own U.S. of promise trailed off on the skyline like a sentence

Which brings us to Egan's personal tribute, his hope that Pound will find the paradise he tried so hard to write in the *Cantos*, his acknowledgement of the debt poets, including himself, owe to Pound: 'these few lines from my time that would have been worse/only for you.' As he pays this tribute, Egan brilliantly compares Pound to Hercules, the hero of Pound's version of Sophocles' *The Women of Trachis*: both men laboured long and hard, both made a fatal mistake (*hamartia*) — Hercules bringing home a new mistress to his wife, Pound supporting Fascism — and paid dearly for it, Hercules accidentally killed by his wife, Pound spending twelve years in the psychiatric hospital. This makes the appearance of Hercules here so apt:

> rest troubled Hercules! your best labours shine like new words
> the remainder as with anyone else doesn't count

4

Egan's elegy for his father Thomas Egan (died 1985), his most sustained and accomplished performance in this genre, consists of a sequence of 18 poems, 'A Song For My Father' (SF 49-61). Although the epigraph to the sequence from E.M. Cioran warns us that poetry, like everything else, cannot ultimately capture experience,[12] Egan, aided by the device of the sub-text in 9 poems, is nevertheless extremely successful both in his portrayal of Tom Egan and of what his father meant to him. While the sequence does not lack a certain narrative framework — we begin in I with the father alive and well, end in XVIII with his epitaph — the dominant narratological device is that of juxtraposition of past and present, out of sequence. This non-chronological approach allows, crucially, the poet to explore with the complexity it requires the vital question of the ontological status of all that is being described. The sequence is fundamentally concerned with the problem of reality, or rather, of a series of realities.

The sequence begins in Poem I with the reality of a family lunch outdoors. Since Egan is a Platonist/Christian, he is able to save the phenomena of this pastoral landscape and grant them their proper ontological status: the summer sun with 'my father in shirtsleeves,' the flowers, the dinner, and most significantly of all, a doll that 'lies forever in the sun.' Egan is indeed seeing all this in a photograph, but such is the power of remembrance and of the emotion aroused by the past occasion that his daughter's doll transcends the passing of time and is preserved not just for that moment, but for always. Here the eternal everyday is what constitutes reality.

In Poem II the pastoral scene is immediately and brutally replaced by the technology of a modern hospital, where the heart of the poet's dying father is being monitored by a machine and where that heart finally stopped beating on 'Wednesday 17 April.' Now the reality that the Platonist must face is that of death that comes to all in this fallen world of 'everyone's utter fragility.'

While the sub-text here also confronts the fact of human suffering and death, it deals too with yet another form of reality, that of the love between father and son which mirrors that of the poet's grandfather for his son and is therefore seen as a vital ingredient in the human condition.

These three forms of reality that are established in the opening two poems — the eternal everyday, death, love — remain central to the rest of the sequence.

What unites poems VI, IX, XI, XII and XIV is that, although they accept the fact of Tom Egan's terminal illness, they also chronicle the times that father and son were together in the past, distant or recent. In XIV as the poet continues to visit his father in hospital 'day/by day by new day,' the sub-text looks for an '*outward sign*' that in better days his father would readily have provided with the detached Midland assertion of the main text '*lookit it doesn't matter a curse*.' At that point main text and sub-text converge to dwell on a precious shared moment from the past when father and son were at their ease and things were normal with customers coming into the shop. Similarly, in poem VI the main text seizes on a moment in the poet's childhood when his father was vigorous and healthy, while the sub-text dwells on the worn, suffering, confused, dying bodies in the hospital.

Poem XII describes the poet driving his father from Mullingar to Athlone as his father had once driven him and recalls their shared past over the years. Because they both know the true situation about the father's health — he is dying — they now have some further shared moments, which ironically include the denial of death by a local priest who placed the inscription '*See you later*' on his gravestone.

But death will not be denied: while the car is 'heading home' to Athlone, this 'turned out our final trip.'

In poem XI the main text sees the poet plant a shrub in his lawn the week his father died to serve as a memorial to the dead man and bring new life in the spring, a form of resurrection of the man whose easy handling of the topic of death when he was alive, graphically recounted in the sub-text, nicely correlates with what he might say when he comes back, '*Take it easy you cod you*,' and prepares the way for his own death. In poem IX the poet, again using nature as a symbol of life, throws a spring daffodil onto his father's grave. But the flower is also linked to the past and to the many shared experiences listed by the poet, taking 'with it part of myself.' Since the daffodil is therefore a complex symbol, it is entirely appropriate that 'I never saw it land.'

There is little consolation in poems IV, V, VI, XIII and XV. In poem V the fact that his father has died means that the poet will no longer be able to join with him in daily experience, specifically in attending Sunday soccer matches in which the Athlone team plays. That these shared events have decisively come to an end is emphasized by the sevenfold anaphora of the nostalgic phrase 'no more,' while the sub-text relating to the hospital underlines this pain by stressing the father's vulnerability.

In poem IV the poet is shocked that his father who is in the intensive care unit of the hospital, begins uncharacteristically to cry 'great shuddering male sobs.' The poet seeks instinctively to protect him, even four months later, but is totally unable to do so, since human pain is inevitable and incurable:

> and even yet
> even this wet windy August day I want
> to throw my arms around you shield you
>
> I who have no shield

Poem XIII takes this pessimism a stage further. The death of the poet's father which is perceived as final — 'all that he was faded away' — has had the catastrophic effect of taking away from the reality of everything that makes up the eternal everyday: 'leaving the whole show less real.' The result is that the quotidian events they enjoyed together, the details of contemporary soccer and of the poet's reception by the media, to which his father would had responded with 'that zest of his,' have lost their meaning, have indeed had their reality radically diminished. Which means that the poet is unable to participate in the same way in these events any more:

> how can I bring myself ever again
> to watch a home match?

Similarly, when in poem XV the poet revisits the hospital in which his father died to thank the staff, the pastoral landscape visible from his father's now empty room — cows, lake, flowers — is at one level familiar, but at another is merely a Platonic shadow of its former self, irrevocably altered by the bleak fact of death, no longer real:

> everything
> pretending to be

There is loss also in poem XVI. After the month's mind Mass for his father, the poet experiences an emptiness in his home, a gap where his father used to be and now is not. An astonishingly original idea describes this loss: whereas at the Mass the family have just attended the bread and wine are changed, 'transubstantiated,' into the body and blood of Christ, the family have been, by a reverse process, changed back into the past, a past itself in the process of dying, a past which is becoming less real in its evanescence:

> we have been
> transubstantiated into the past
> and even the past is dying

There is, however, another side of the coin: consolation in one form or another.

Two poems in the sequence, III and VIII, recall the past without any sense of loss. In VIII in the main text the poet's father goes for a walk down the street, meeting various people on the way, and we must recall that this 'ordinary fella' is engaged in precious activity in 'the metaphysical street.' In the sub-text we have another vignette from vibrant, everyday life with the poet's father sitting down after Sunday dinner and laughing, while he waits for his cup of tea. Similarly, in poem III, although the father is 'in the intensive care unit where he lay dying,' the poet is convinced of the value of that ebbing life — 'how valiant his life its shape' — which is a model for himself and so expresses his love for his father like the local river Shannon flooding its banks:

> for the first time since I put on long trousers I
> kissed my father
>
> *flood*
> *its*
> *banks*

For the Christian there is consolation in the shape of life after death and, making use of Christ's dictum 'In my father's house are many mansions,'[13] Egan considers in poem X which mansion his father, 'no intellectual,' might be found in. Using the device of the priamel,[14] in which we are presented with a series of initial topics, termed the foil, before we come to the real, central topic, termed the climax, Egan rules out in succession the mansions inhabited by philosophers, poets, politicians, and musicians. This brings us to the grove in Elysium that would appeal to his father, the one inhabited by the local people of Athlone who drink tea, go for a walk, and talk about their native place or about football. Once more ordinary life, because it is preferred to political, intellectual and artistic endeavor and because it is nevertheless granted a place in Heaven, has been recognized as having the status of metaphysical reality.

We come to the last two poems of the sequence, XVII and XVIII. In XVII the mood of the main text, as the poet and his mother visit Tom Egan's grave, is despondent, nature at first conspiring in the atmosphere of death and then becoming a symbol of transience. For the budding flowers and warm grass of poem I have turned into:

> our bouquets stripped to wire
>
> and leaves like years
> lodged in the sodden grass

The sub-text tells a different story. The poet, unlike the mother, does not cry, because he believes that it is only the physical remains of his father that lie in the grave and that his real self is in another realm of existence: '*my father is elsewhere.*'

There lies the possibility of consolation. With the result that in the last poem of the sequence, privileged not only by its position, but also by being only one of two granted a title and that the significantly summarizing 'Epitaph,' Egan turns apparent reality on its head by denying the fact of death, by exchanging the classic formula *hic iacet Thomas Egan* for the opposing, bare, emphatic 'Tom Egan does not lie here.' Death is indeed denied by the five negatives found in the six-line poem (including a threefold anaphora of 'not') and the corresponding stress on the opposites to death, on the father's warmth, laugh, spirit, on the love of his family for him. Ultimately, it is that 'love more lasting than granite' — a phrase that transposes Horace's boast about his poetry to human love[15] — that is the guarantee that death does not end all, that, as Propertius says, *traicit et fati litora magnus amor*.[16] In the ontological stakes for Egan, as for Dante, love is the only true reality.

FIVE

Je T'Aime: Love Poetry

1

The manifold achievements of Anglo-Irish poetry in this century can hardly be said to include a substantial body of love poetry. The reason for this lacuna no doubt relates to the overwhelming feeling in twentieth century Anglo-Irish literature of sexual loss. This is often attributed to the dictates of puritanical religion, so that from O Faoláin to McGahern, from O'Connor to Harding, the clash between sexuality and religion in the form of Jansenistic Catholicism has been remorselessly chronicled and has resulted in the phenomenon dubbed by Augustine Martin 'inherited dissent.'[1]

Love poetry, writing that deals with *both* success *and* failure in sexual love is rare and even in the one great sequence of love poems in modern Anglo-Irish literature, that of Yeats, the theme is almost totally that of unrequited love. It is of course true that poems of unhappy love are more prevalent in literature than poems of happy love. It is sufficient to consider the exemplary case of Catullus, founder of European love poetry and recorder of his disastrous passion for Lesbia, and to ponder on Byron's dictum:

> Think you, if Laura had been Petrarch's wife,
> He would have written sonnets all his life?[2]

In the work of Desmond Egan,[3] however, we encounter poems both of unhappy and of happy love. In *Leaves* (1974) upon the landscape mapped-out earlier in *Midland*, we find superimposed the theme of an unhappy love affair with an emphasis on loss; in *Snapdragon* (1983), on the other hand, the emphasis is on requited love. Significantly though, *Snapdragon* owes allegiance not to Anglo-Irish literature, but rather to literature written in the Irish language and to continental poetry such as that of Machado, Neruda, and Akhmatova. So Egan's poetry is linked with the Gaelic tradition of celebrating love — which chimes with that of the troubadours of Provence and their successors; as James Liddy puts it:

> . . . with your Gaelic libido
> you want to sing a song of Normandy —
> Provence.[4]

2

Egan has said in an interview that 'Where *Midland* is landscape, *Leaves* is
figures in a landscape and maybe one figure in particular.'[5] So *Leaves*, whose
title programmatically establishes a link between the world of nature —
leaves falling from trees — and the personal — the notion of leaving or
parting — deals with the theme of separation, of loss.

Written in his discursive manner, the major and richly satisfying title poem
'Leaves' (CP 64-65) brings together some of the themes touched-upon in the
book. As in so many other poems, the changing processes of nature mirror
those of human beings; as in Horace's *Odes* (for example 1.23-25) spring is
the time for life and love, winter the time for death and abandonment. In the
opening poem of *Leaves*, 'Along the Boyne,' nature is beneficent for the
lovers as they walk together; in the next poem, 'Leaves,' it is more of a
negative counterbalance as they part.

Two key images from nature — leaves and the river — convey graphically
the notion that the relationship is over: as the leaves fallen from the trees in
autumn float in the river Liffey in Dublin, so the affair is at an end. Both these
images symbolize what is transitory in human life; Homer has told us (*Iliad*
6.146), 'as are the generations of leaves, so are the generations of men'; water
is the archetypal symbol of flux in Heraclitus, and of mutable, generated
matter in Neoplatonism. At the very beginning of the poem we read of 'the
Liffey running/with leaves' — contrasting with 'and the Liffey stood,'
applied to a time of happiness in the poem 'Close To You' — and five of the
paragraphs end with a refrain in italics, which in all five occurrences refers
to the river and in four of them to the leaves as well, firmly insisting with ever
more urgency on the ephemeral nature of things. The refrain begins with the
river running, and moves on successively to the river running 'with leaves,'
'heavy with leaves,' and 'with all the leaves' until the final climactic
occurrence in which the irrevocable ending of the affair is seen to be the cause
of the death of all that is attractive in nature:

it chokes the river on all the bright leaves

But there is much more in 'Leaves' than this schematic outline. The
opening paragraph sees the protagonist driving along the Quays in Dublin,
and establishes a precise geographical location. Immediately the image of
the woman comes to mind as a dramatic epiphany and brings 'joy' —
incidentally a key word in troubadour poetry, e.g. that of Bernard de
Ventador. But joy is problematic because the Liffey, unlike the snowdrop in
the poem 'P.S.,' does not link the lovers — it is 'unwhispering' — but rather

53

stresses the fleeting nature of things, river and beloved being related through the use of italics, a stress emphasized by the refrain which sounds ominously for the first time.

Consequently, there is a distinctly poignant air about the tensions of the second paragraph. Here we read of how the beloved is not, as always, a source of delight; of how she causes fever in the wrong season, autumn; of how she does '*exist*,' the italics again paradoxically linking her to the river and so to flux; and, finally, of how the very page of the poem itself is identified with 'this leaf,' now a symbol of flowering and growth. Despite these tensions, the epiphany is genuine and in the third paragraph various physical and emotional facets of the beloved, which belong properly to summer, like a tree full of leaves, are mentioned; indeed the impact of the girl reasserts itself at the moment of writing — but the fragile nature of such thoughts is once more underlined by the recurrence of the refrain, now embracing both symbols of flux: river and leaves.

The first explicit assertion that the relationship have failed occurs in the fourth paragraph. There is a tension between the phrases that make this assertion — they are in parentheses — and the identification of the beloved with the happy, smiling past of the poet which 'will not fall old.' Which gives us in the fifth paragraph the paradox that, even if she leaves the poet physically, she can never leave emotionally; her status as that second person, as *you*, *tu*, *du*, the other half of himself, will never change to the impersonal third person, *she*; that goodbye is, in a real sense, not goodbye at all. This thought leads to a vivid recall of happy moments in the past, the woman's enthusiasm, the girl singing in the summer, smiling even though she is going away. But then the refrain obtrudes itself again with its message of change and defeat; the river now full of leaves, the happy moments gone.

The sixth paragraph begins by contrasting the behavior of the girl now that all is autumn: she turns away, in youthful disregard. The tone once more modulates, so that her beautiful hair is both a physical phenomenon and evocative of the spirit or even of a dream. In turn, this is again undercut by the refrain, which now ominously speaks of '*all the leaves*.'

This brings us in paragraph seven to the last meeting of the lovers in the Shelbourne Hotel in Dublin. The woman leaves and her departure brings about a change in the status of things: the sofa they sat on becomes a Platonic shadow, the dress of summer an ironic echo, and the poem moves to its conclusion with two two-line paragraphs, which sum up the situation like epigrams:

> because you will sit busily in its open door
> leaning across in a dazzle   again never
>
> 'forever'
> *it chokes*
>   *the river*
>   *on all the bright leaves*

In the second paragraph the single, final emphatic 'forever,' stressing the irrevocable nature of the separation, is immediately underlined by the refrain, which is no longer in tension with the main text, but which rather emphasizes the definitive nature of the parting: all their previous happy times are, once and for all, over. There is no more to be said.

3

A number of other poems in the volume *Leaves* deal with the relationship whose end is chronicled in 'Leaves.' Some inkling of why the relationship finished is provided by the poem '(Wait river speak and o speak...' (CP 68). Here the woman questions the basis of a relationship, beginning with a query about what core element within her the man is pursuing. His answer is very unsatisfactory, since he professes ignorance coupled with a tentative reference to her 'sureness,' which is immediately undermined by associating this quality with water, symbol of flux.

In her second intervention the girl confesses that she is subject to perpetual mood swings, *varium et mutabile semper/femina (Aeneid* 4. 569-70):

> *But Listen!*
> *I'm never calm I'm*
> *pure flesh I'm mood-changing*
> *each single breath*

Faced with this, the speaker has to reconsider. He decides that she is right, and uses the changing faces of nature — the swaying weeds, the beech that sheds its leaves — as analogue for such swings of moods. This traumatic insight leads him to apostrophize both nature and humans, before coming to the final rhetorical question:

>   and what could I say
> as she
> turned her way?

The answer is 'nothing', and the distance between the two, literal and metaphorical, is stressed by the typography, which keeps 'I' and 'she' apart on the page, while the apparent rhyme of say/way mocks the notion that the lovers do in fact coincide. Their relationship is therefore in a state of flux like a river and this gives us the meaning of the poem's title.

By the time of 'The Tunnels of June' (CP 70) the woman has left. The poem uses the image of the speaker driving a car along a road overhung with trees as a metaphor to describe his relationship with the woman in the heady month of June.

The emphatic repetition of the verb 'drove' stresses the intensity of his commitment, but a note of warning about the brilliant light and endless, luxuriant scenes of this green and pleasant land is soon sounded: for there is an emphasis on 'struggling' in 'this otherworld' and an aposiopesis concerning what is 'lost,' which, together with the further hint of 'notes,' suggests the myth of Orpheus and Eurydice, whose relationship came to an abrupt end when Orpheus, having persuaded Persephone by his music to let his wife go, looked back at Eurydice with the result that she vanished.

After all the pleasures of June, the woman disappears without warning. Consequently, the final, climactic three lines of the poem rewrite Burns's assertion 'My love is like a red red rose/ That's newly sprung in June,'[6] so that the rose near the woman's window is linked not to love, but to water and so flux, and the woman has vanished as Eurydice did from Orpheus:

> a soaked rose
> deepened above the gravel streaming
> by her orphic window

In 'If' (CP 92) there is a bracing to accept that the affair is over. Despite the fact that the title of the poem is 'If' and that the conjunction 'if' occurs six times (in each case of the beginning of the line), only a minimum of doubt is being expressed about the statements made in this series of protases: the OED tells us that when the protasis of a conditional clause is in the indicative mood — here the phrase 'I don't,' repeated six times — the speaker may accept the truth of the statement in the clause.[7] In fact, then the if-clauses here, like *si*-clauses in Latin, do not imply any major doubt about what is being stated, but express confidence that the assertions made are true. So we have a succession of assertions about what the poet does not now do and, since all these statements relate to the past, he is providing a comprehensive account of how the relationship is over.

What the speaker no longer exhibits, then, is an obsession with the beloved. Yet the very act of listing his forms of obsession adds a note of ambiguity:

he *is*, in one sense, still obsessed and the final line summarises this:

> this is my first goodbye

Nevertheless, the relationship is over because 'I don't need you any more,' though this lack of concern has been won at enormous cost, vividly proclaimed in a brilliant simile:

> — it's because I have forced myself to learn
> practising bitterly like a failed athlete
> not to care anymore no more

Two other poems, 'Close to you . . .' and 'September Dandelion,' show the lovers' closeness to be extremely fragile. In 'Close to you . . .' (CP 73), whose title is that of a pop song by Perry Como, the protagonist hears the song on a car radio — as it happens, quite near the Hill of Allen (itself associated with Oisín, the mythical hero brought by Niamh to Tír na nÓg). This is not his type of music and yet it has a considerable effect upon him, making him sad because of its past associations and ensuring that he rapidly and lugubriously recalls the past. He remembers, in particular, the times he and the woman were together in what now seems a separate country of its own, like Oisín's *Tír na nÓg*, a past in which they piled-up activities that would provide material for a large number of books (like *Leaves*) and in which the river Liffey, now a symbol of flux, then marked a kind of stability, a stability that contrasts with rapidly flowing memories:

> somewhere I didn't know inside
> so ulcerous sad
> (everything was running by
> like the Country where we made
> books and books
>
> and the Liffey stood)

Because of this mood, the speaker angrily recalls another specific occasion when he was on his way to rocky Connemara. but that was in the distant past and, just as Oisín grew old and died when he returned from Tír na nÓg, so this other lover has experienced a type of death, in which his past life rushes before his eyes and he is left, like Yeats, with 'nothing but memories':[8]

I had to
smash my fist at the air

of another time (hundreds of hours ago)
speeding to the stone West

one white horse chasing the waves

This fragility in a relationship is also captured in the immediately preceding poem, 'September Dandelion' (CP 72). It is autumn. The dandelion of summer is a phenomenon now firmly rooted in the past and has to be *remembered*, just as in 'Close to you . . .' It mirrors a fragile situation, one made explicit by the old ritual of blowing off seeds of the flower to the accompaniment of the refrain *'She loves me/She loves me not — .'* The dandelion is about to disintegrate, to blow to pieces, and this process is likely to begin at any time. The inference is that the relationship is equally fragile and likely to break down at any moment; even so insubstantial a thing as a breath will bring about this result:

to break
blowing a little by the roadside
any move now

any breath

Things, however, were not always so fraught and some poems recall happier moments. As 'Along the Boyne' (CP 63), the opening poem of *Leaves* and programmatic to the extent that it concerns the lovers and links them to nature. Whereas the opening title poem of *Midland* deals almost entirely with nature and no living person enters directly, the opening poem of *Leaves* begins straightway with another person: the beloved 'you,' and goes on to include 'I,' the protagonist. Indeed the verbs predicated of the two people — 'you went ahead'; 'I followed' — indicate a relationship which is essentially satisfactory at this point, though they are slightly apart; for the two are walking in harmony, both literally and metaphorically; as Catullus puts it, *cum ventitabas quo puella ducebat.*[9]

The scene of this harmonious walk, upon which the girl is launched at the very beginning of the poem, is a path beside the river Boyne. Nature is here described in a mainly favorable way, at one with the lovers in its richness and peace: lush foliage, the river flowing in its eternal way, the Boyne river, mother of the salmon of knowledge. There are some discordant notes: 'the entaglement of gases,' 'one blooded poppy' — but the scene is one of love in secluded, idyllic surroundings, when even the woman's clothes relate to nature: 'the flowered gown.' But as the speaker prepares to join the smiling girl at the end of the path, there is a hint, a warning, a sting:

> nettle-burned thumb still to your lips
> waiting   where the path stopped

In 'P.S.' (CP 84) the nature theme continues, as the author encloses a snowdrop in a letter he has written. The season is spring when 'a young man's fancy lightly turns to thoughts of love':[10] he has just written a letter and while the poem really constitutes a postscript to that letter, it is, of course, a love poem. The burden is that the writer has inserted a snowdrop between the pages of his letter, an early flowering snowdrop with its white pendant flower, which in 'Not on the course' is a symbol of spring and in 'Almost February' is linked to love of life. This snowdrop is lightly particularized since it was just picked from a bunch of flowers in front of a house known to them both.

Despite the fact that flowers don't travel well and that the snowdrop will arrive 'crushed bedraggled,' the speaker is intent on sending it and hopes she will not be disappointed at its condition. The snowdrop, symbol of spring, functions as a direct personal link between lover and beloved: personified and attributed a soul, it is permeated by the morning dew, which literally touches the words of the letter and transforms them metaphorically, so that a message comes from the soul of the flower to the woman, whose own hands are at one with the spring. Once again, nature is benign:

> listen   a snow soul
> may whisper something
>
> that its dew full of the evening
> will have spread through my words
>
> when you open them in your
> spring hands

4

In *Woodcutter*, published four years after *Leaves*, the poems 'Sunday evening' and 'Under London' look back nostalgically on the relationship. In 'Sunday evening' (CP 127), one of Egan's most successful love poems, the speaker walks on a Dublin beach and thinks of a time when the woman was with him there. Concern is stressed by the device of the priamel, in which a number of other matters are mentioned first in order to highlight the real theme of the poem, which only fully emerges later:

> hands in jeans along Dollymount I don't see
> the slow line of the wave breaking far
> out under Howth in mist a Tír na nÓg I don't see
> the long strand quiet as another sky
> nor the seasun the wrack dead things a saturated beam
>
> — but you who are not there
> sitting any more legs crossed on a sand dune
> picking at chips with musical fingers to laugh
> deeper than the wine that *This is LOVE-ly*
> while the sparse grass blows
>
> forever as I pass

In contrast with Stephen Dedalus in *Ulysses* who strongly emphasizes the 'ineluctable modality of the visible,' the speaker ignores the coast of Howth to the north and the long strand he is now on, with its desolate seaweed and jetsam; instead, he dwells on the beloved as she once was on this strand, pictures her in an idyllic scene in which nature, far from being desolate, was benign, and at which the woman rejoiced, using even the word 'love.' But the poem ends with another aspect of nature, its permanence, which is in stark contrast with the transitory of human beings; as Horace says (*Odes* 4.7.13-16), *damna tamen celeres reparant caelestia lunae:/nos ubi decidimus/ . . . pulvis et umbra sumus.*

In 'Under London' (CP 126) the woman, now living in London is recalled again. From one point of view, she is close at hand but from another unattainable in this vast city. No point in looking for her; what can be done, as always, is to *remember*, for it is memory that guaranteees the reality of what has happened — in the memorable phrase, 'it/becomes fully real only by memory' ('Under London') or, as Pound puts it (after Cavalcanti), 'dove sta memoria.'[11]

So we have a nostalgic list of items from that past, many of them presented in other poems in *Leaves*: the girl 'singing with June' and 'that Boyne hair . . . flying' in 'Leaves'; the closeness of the lovers in 'Along the Boyne'; wine and chips in 'Sunday evening'; music in 'Close to you'; letters in 'P.S.'; in a word, the 'misery/and sheer joy' that is so eloquently evoked in *Leaves*.

Now all that has come to an end, as ephemeral as the relationship, at this moment, of the tent to the Hackney marshes in London. Consequently, memory is almost the final guarantor of what is real and at the very end it too faces away and a sudden imaginative shift leaves us a terrible vision of utter transience:

> the track where a tent has stood
>
> the Hackney marshes

5

The superb volume *Snapdragon* (1983) consists entirely of a sequence of 12 love poems and reminds us again that Egan tends to publish sequences rather than individual poems. Although, as always, there is a keen awareness of loss and of the possibility of loss there is here also happiness. In fact the volume acknowledges the complexity of human love, which cannot be reduced to formulae, not least by refusing a separate title to 10 of the 12 poems, of which he uses the first line as title. This device adds weight to a line and establishes a mood (an analogy might be made with the relevance of size in painting). A further indication of complexity is the appropriation at the beginning of the volume of three poems in Irish — the first a traditional song, whose nuances have defied translation, the other two, translations by the contemporary poets Tomás MacSíomóin and Douglas Sealy. We have moved away from the endless whining about lost love that characterizes so much Anglo-Irish literature in this century to a more mature recognition of what is involved.

The opening poem of *Snapdragon*, 'The South Wind' (CP 168-69), chimes with the poems of loss in the volume *Leaves*. Like *Leaves*, the poem discovers in nature a symbol of what is happening in human life. So the wind, associated with winter and with transience, has detached the girl, who is equated with the summer month of July, with the sun, dawn, and lark. The protagonist is equated with a cloud blown by the wind.

That is, of course, one possible scenario, but there are many poems of happy love in *Snapdragon*. The most explicit of these is the poem 'Je t'aime' (CP 179). Here the opening assertion in French derives its force from the fact that is gives something like a real title to the poem and that the familiar form of the second person has a resonance that the English 'I love you' lacks. After the frost of winter, inimical to love, the snowdrop, reminder of spring and of love, cannot be far behind; and the Greek for 'I love you' (which continues the connection with Continental Europe) underlines the message. But the Greek has also another function, since it suggests the noun *agapé*, which refers to the love feasts of the early Christians and so prepares the way for the linking that immediately follows of love with the infinite.

Since love is transcendent, the beloved will obviously elude definition, the formula of words. This failure of language is stressed by the image of the fisherman, whose narrow net cannot encompass either the passion or the calm of a human being. Then follows a description of the effect which the beloved has, in images acknowledged as inadequate. One of these indeed — that of the 'broken firmament' — mirrors the fragmented nature of thought and feeling. On the other hand, when the beloved — now addressed in German, *liebchen* — is there, it is easy to describe her impact. She suggests the infinite, ensuring that we have now moved beyond the ordinary flowers of spring, like the snowdrop, beyond German love-lieder (as in 'Morning in wind and new sounds'), beyond the four Indo-European languages found in this poem . . . have moved into an entirely different realm of experience onto a higher, transcendent level:

> but when you turn my way *liebchen* so easily
> things begin flowering strangely outwards toward
> unheard songs the primary colours of a new
> unspoken language . . .

In Egan's poetry, as we have seen, so often, nature mirrors the world of human beings and, in particular, the ups and downs of love. But in the poem 'Mislaying losing leaving yourself behind' (CP 176) human intervention *creates*, in the image of the woman as expert gardener, the flowers and plants of love. This creation constitutes a spontaneous emanation and so merits terms like 'generosity,' 'extravagance,' 'rich.' What it means is that everyday things of one kind or another are forgotten in favour of this powerful outflow. The creation affects the poet's inmost being, his soul, so that it discovers facets of which he was unaware, and, at a quotidian level, his approach to life — so e.g. that he greatly admires the way the woman can dismiss material considerations. The creator's fingers are green in the usual metaphorical sense of producing abundant flowers, but, since the flowers symbolize life, the fingers also produce love:

> only a rich soul
> could sow such after images and
>
> under the extravagance of those green fingers
> love grows love

The transforming effect of love is found also in the poem 'And sometimes you are in everything' (CP 181). If hope is the virtue chronicled in 'Morning in wind and new sounds'; and love, that found in 'Je t'aime'; the virtue recorded in this poem is faith. At times the experiences of loss is dominant

— as in 'Why is it that your *ave atque vale*'; in this poem, fulfilment is the central theme. This fullness arises out of a belief that, at times, the beloved is 'in everything,' a force transforming all aspects of existence. The radical nature of this transforming force can be seen in her power to charge with possibilities not merely those things like fields and bridges that might be expected to chime with love, but also those phenomena of nature like a river and autumn that (as we have often seen) are reminders of transience and of vulnerability.

So the first place associated with the beloved is a river which, though long, is 'unmoving' and reminds us that, in happy times, 'the Liffey stood'; the river is therefore now an exemplar not of the Heraclitean dictum that all is in flux, but rather, of a mood that transforms everything.

Again, the beloved ensures that the 'hollow afternoon sounds' of 'Through flurries of wind and the rain' are metamorphosed into sounds from the town and the schoolyard that are positive. More: within the idyllic, pastoral landscape of the Midlands she embraces the totality of nature's cycles: 'the green intenseness of fields' *and* 'trees beginning to say *autumn*'; flowers that bloom and fade; the weir that both restrains *and* releases water.

The poem goes on to conclude with her guaranteeing the very reality of 'whatever is real.' So the new bridge leads not to the restriction of 'hills I never needed to reach,' but opens the way to wonderful, faraway hills and we are no longer dealing with morning or afternoon or night, but with 'the whole day,' with all of reality. The power of love is limitless.

The key concept in the poem 'Morning in wind and new sounds' (CP 177) is that of hope. Morning brings fresh and gently hopeful sounds which contrast with the 'hollow afternoon sounds' of 'Through flurries of wind and the rain' and with 'the night barks' of 'Crows are clamouring on the low roof.' Then we immediately go to thoughts about the beloved and to one of the most explicit professions found in this sequence:

> morning in wind and new sounds
> morning of the mild echo of the heart
> my thoughts fill with your hopefulness go
> cradling a faraway sleeping life one
> more precious than my own the
> all that tenderly she is

In the midst of this avowal come three lines of a German lied — words by John Henry Mackay for music by Richard Strauss — that universalise the theme of love. As often in Egan, nature here mirrors love, so that the sunshine is an analogue for the closeness of the lovers and the prevailing sentiment is

63

that of hope which leads to the assertion that love goes beyond any feeling he has for anything else; as Catullus puts it, *mihi quae me carior ipso est.*[12] This deep love at first seems to transcend even ongoing hopes — but then love and hope become virtually interchangeable so that there is a direct identification of the beloved with hope itself.

The poem then returns in ring composition to morning, greeted like a welcome friend and reminding us of the simple joy of 'this day this fresh time.' Morning will, in due course, give way to the afternoon of an autumn that, in contrast to the threatening autumn of 'Through flurries of wind and the rain,' brings with it hope: hope that the beloved will return; hope underlined by the final, evocative word 'open.'

One further poem in the sequence, 'Mystery which I never want to solve' (CP 170-71) is also positive about love. The first real poem of the sequence begins appropriately with the key word 'mystery': love is not amenable to purely rational analysis and the speaker is happy that this should be so. This mystery manifests itself in the woman, as hard to pin down as aspects of nature such as the horizon and mist. Both nature and woman are mysterious, which means there are questions that cannot be asked.

Any thought that the man can cut himself free is to be rejected because the woman's destiny has now become his as well — fact emphasized by the term of endearment *a ghrá* (this also makes us look back at the original text in Irish). The result is that the lovers experience a common fortune that pleases the man (it gives us the only punctuation, an exclamation mark, in the poem — 'ours!'). Given their shared life, the voice of the beloved involves trees, but the leaves here are not — as in the volume *Leaves* and especially in the title poem 'Leaves' — a symbol of the transient but rather, since new leaves will replace the old, of renewal; again, that other reminder of transience, the river, is involved here in the union of the lovers. In that union the beloved, conceived of in terms of warmth and light, has an apotropaic function, warding off dreams of loss, darkness, and cold. The poem therefore closes with the poet calling the woman like the head of a sleeping person:

> I will try to cradle you to me like a river to
> ward off with my life all the nightmares of falling
> and the dance of the dark the cold
>
> to draw you gently as a sleeping head
> into the arm where we can dream again together

6

Snapdragon is not always so positive; other poems deal with loss. In the first of these, 'Crows are clamouring on the low roof' (CP 172-73), the woman has left after a quarrel and the poem is about loneliness. On a train speeding away, the beloved with her 'normal sounds' has been replaced by the disruptive, raucous cawing of crows. The salient feature of every room in the cottage is that she is not there. Even worse, the man realizes that she will now make a radical reassessment, with the result that he feels alienated from his environment, threatened by everything:

> ... I know
>
> you are figuring me out again: that
> judgement tender and cruel as youth
>
> making me become now a
> burglar even in my own house
> so that everything begins to scream its otherness
> and the night barks
> barks

The protagonist then addresses her directly and the poem takes a different turn. He calls her *mignonne*, a French term of endearment. The only hope now is that she who is related to light and to life (as in Catullus) will return and guarantee normality. Since *amantium irae amoris integratio est*,[13] what is required is simply the word from her that *'it's all right.'* With that statement she will assert her nature, one inseparable from the celebration of life. Symbolized in the last line by music.

The next poem, 'Through flurries of wind and the rain' (CP 174), sees the man aiming at reconciliation. Once more nature acts as moral metaphor. The summer has gone and now the clouds and winds of autumn, of September, mean that leaves and rain are everywhere. As rain is emphatically equated with defeat, a break is suggested. Some similarity between this poem and those in *Leaves* should not blind us to the fact that the tone here is different: whereas the break between man and woman is irrevocable in *Leaves*, here it is only temporary. Consequently, there is considerable stress on the statement 'I/am reaching again for you,' which is repeated at the beginning and end of the poem, bracketing the rest of it. (Attend to the word 'again.')

Now the theme of memory recurs, but is handled differently. In poems like 'Under London' what is remembered is set firmly in the past and concerns what is finally ended; in this poem there is still the possibility of reunion: what is remembered is set in the present and may in fact not be remembered at all — because the answer to two rhetorical questions in paragraphs three and four seems to be 'no.' Consequently, the river and sycamore leaves, though undoubtedly redolent of flux (as so often), do not deliver (as they do in 'Leaves') a definitive verdict that the relationship is over: the drabness of the world; the meaninglessness of sounds (in contrast to the 'normal sounds' of 'Crows are clamouring on the low roof'); a child crying, constitute symbols of a temporary break. There is no Poundian *memoria* here.

'Your tears will not dry' (CP 175) is about a sad moment that cannot be redeemed. It is a poem about time — past, present, future — and the timeless. The first three paragraphs deal in a complex way with the future and assert that the unhappiness of the woman, represented by falling tears and quivering lips, a *datum* for which no explanation is given, will not cease in that future. Futhermore, she will remain silent, a state related to stagnant water. On the other hand, her concern will also remain constant: this concern affirmed in the injunction '*Look after yourself*' can never be unsaid, words to express her loneliness can never be articulated.

The poem then moves to the past. The woman has experienced many empty rooms — compare the man in 'Crows are clamouring on the low roof.' This leads to a rhetorical question that expects the answer 'yes':

> beloved were you paying for my fantasies?

Now, in the present, the speaker will try to make amends. He will in fact transcend time and make timeless statements, which will doubtless include a profession of love. This love can be equated with the marigold that also transcends time and does not die, because flowers, as the poem 'P.S.' has taught us, have a soul, souls are immortal — and all the more so, when the flower in question is named after the Virgin Mary, and after the most precious of metals, gold, which does not rust. So while future and past are problematical, the present has immortality in it:

> but grasping the latch into the present
> I want to whisper with all my life the
> things which are timeless
> to remind you that no marigold dies

Two other poems — 'Like coals you settle' (CP 178) and 'Why is it that your *ave atque vale*' (CP 180) — which come just before and after 'Je t'aime' — deal with the theme of loss. Whereas in the poem 'Your tears will not dry' the man could not hope to warm any rooms for the beloved, in 'Like coals you settle,' the woman, equated in a simile with burning coals, causes the fierce heat of confusion, despair, and misery to flare up in his mind. Since absence makes the heart grow fonder, these emotions are aroused 'after you have just left' and indicate the loneliness he feels. Indeed separation here has a feeling of finality about it and leads to a sense of winter and to nostalgic recall of the summer, a season of love, with its luxuriant snapdragons along the house front. The image of the snapdragons is crucial because it provides the title for the whole volume and clearly its rich evocativeness includes love. The poem does not end with nostalgic recall of the past; rather, there is the promise of further human contact, as the phone 'gets ready to ring.'

In 'Why is it that your *ave atque vale*' we encounter a fallen world, its Babel suggested by the use of two further languages, Latin and Spanish, in which the speaker has to contend with temporary separation and wonders why their partings affect him so much. Here the phrase *ave atque vale* from Catullus 101 strikes a very sombre note, since Catullus in that famous poem bids his final hail and farewell to his much-loved dead brother. Again, separation emphasizes the negative side of the man's personality, the Jungian shadow. Keeping to the European tradition via one of the Romance derivatives of Latin, Spanish, the poet continues to worry about loss and its meaning:

> *amada mia* can you explain
> why should the heart at such times begin
> singing in its husky voice the songs of loss?

The poem does not end on that note. Instead the beloved makes an appearance, as part of the rich tapestry of life. What is important, finally, is not her absence (the *vale*), but her presence and commitment to life (the *ave*). This presence, this commitment, and not generalities of whatever kind, constitutes her answer to the rhetorical questions posed in the poem.

7

Now to the last poem of the sequence, 'Dernier Espoir (CP 182):

> coax me from those empty streets
> the dark alleyways I seem to carry
>
> best to my better self
>
> back *ma belle* towards
> the mornings I can almost write
> in letters scrawled big as yours
> as years
>
> turn your words again
> into the locks of my eyes
>
> yes

67

That the poem is assigned a title is in itself significant and means that the protagonist commits himself to this final, defined moment. The title 'Dernier Espoir' is that of a late love poem by Verlaine, the last line of which also provides the epigraph here: 'at least say I live in your heart.' The poem therefore addresses itself to the beloved, as the phrase *ma belle* — also from Verlaine — serves to underline.

Egan's poem is considerably less pessimistic than Verlaine's and, unlike it, envisages a re-union. As always, however, loss or its possibility is round the corner and the speaker feels he had to be enticed away from the negative parts of himself, the Jungian shadow represented by empty streets and dark alleyways. This process of integration with 'my better self' can be achieved only through the lady's good offices — she has herself already fully achieved integration ('best'). That positive side of the poet is suggested by 'morning,' the time of day that affirms life. Enjoined again to speak, the woman utters words of such power that they, paradoxically, become visible, with the result that he seizes them with his eyes.

The poem then ends with a one-word line of affirmation, a simple, emphatic 'yes' that recalls the end of *Ulysses* and guarantees an acceptance of life and love, which is very different from the tentative question that ends Verlaine's poem. For all the talk of loss, Egan ends his sequence on a wholly positive note.

SIX

Too Little Peace: Political Poetry

1

Political poetry is inherently problematical for two basic reasons. Firstly, from Hellenistic times on there have rarely been close links between the poet and the community, so that poets tend to be torn between the pull of articulating their private vision and that of involvement in society, a tension acknowledged by Egan in the poem 'Needing the Sea' (CP 185-86). Secondly, even if poets do write poetry about politics, they run the risk of lapsing into propaganda of one kind or another; as Egan says, 'Propaganda and poetry are two different things, poetry searching for absolute truth, while propaganda tries to promote the discovery of relative ones.'[1] The resolution of these difficulties suggests the beginnings of a programme: political poetry that includes both the individual person and society at large; political poetry that respects the ambiguities and complexities of human affairs.

In meeting these twin goals, political poetry will, necessarily, use language to produce what Shklovsky calls *defamiliarization* (Russian *ostranenie*).[2] Serious prose or poetry claims our attention partly because it uses language in a way that is radically different from conventional, everyday usage, and, in so doing, demands that we reexamine, look anew, at things that may have seemed familiar. This, in turn, requires that we reassess the way we evaluate these things. As might be expected, the central device through which language achieves defamiliarization is metaphor — which itself can best be analysed by means of generative grammar, by postulating the systematic rules that govern usage in a particular language and by then investigating how it is that metaphor breaks the normal selectional rules of that language.[3]

For political poetry in the late twentieth century further complications obtrude: the ability of certain powerful politicians to destroy the kosmos as we know it with nuclear weapons; the massive imbalance of resources between the developed nations and the Third World, resulting in large-scale poverty and the constant threat of famine; and repression by dictatorships — rightwing, leftwing, military, whatever — on a scale that has rarely been equalled and never surpassed. Faced with all of this, there is much to be said for Egan's dictum that 'politics is mostly impotence in drag' (CP 194). But we and he cannot leave it at that, for there is a moral imperative that demands a response, a response that will, by definition, be *negative*, in the sense that it attacks the manifold injustices that now pervade the world. Such a view is endorsed by members of the Frankfurt school such as Adorno, who regard art as the only sphere in which totalitarian rule can be resisted.[4]

Egan's political poetry does, I suggest, meet the challenges outlined. The poems vigorously attack the injustice of corrupt dictatorships; emphasize the disastrous effects of this injustice on the individual person; acknowledge, particularly in regard to Ireland, the ambiguities of political situations; and the use of language is, at all times, radically defamiliarizing. The result is that it is difficult to find any contemporary Irish poet who could stand comparison with Egan in this area.

2

Egan's political poetry is cohesive in theme, but for purposes of analysis it is useful to divide it into three subject areas, to be considered in the next three sections of this essay: Ireland, North and South; the First and Second Worlds (the United States, the Soviet Union, Germany, Japan); and the Third World (Chile, the Falklands, the Philippines, South Africa).

But first a general poem about the state of the world in 1986 entitled 'Peace 1986' (PP 27-28); it is subsequently called simply 'Peace' (SF 38-39).

The undoubted power of this poem derives largely from its use of the formal device called the priamel. In this device (as we have seen), we are presented with a series of initial topics, termed the foil, before we come to the real, central topic, termed the climax; and the structural function of the foil is to place very great emphasis on the climax. In 'Peace' the initial topics of the foil are nature and human participation in it. The details of the landscape in the Irish Midlands — trees, hills, birds — and of the people who walk and live there — parents and a baby, neighbors in a bungalow — function as moral metaphor for normal human life that is peaceful: 'under the deep trees/which whisper of peace'; 'and baby fingers asleep.'

Not, you might think, too much to ask for: 'just that!' But as we move into the climax, the poet invokes Christ to witness that His crown of thorns, symbol of the Crucifixion, has been transferred to the world we live in and that therefore 'that/is more than most of mankind can afford.' Why? Because of the devastating catalogue of injustices that constitue the climax proper, presented with great insistence by means of absolute asyndeton and the tenfold anaphora of the phrase 'too many.' For there are too many countries that do not enjoy the fertility of Ireland, where poverty and famine are rife, too many countries where dictatorships use the security forces to jail and torture people.

We in the developed world are not innocent in this: we are radically diminished at both a mundane and a philosophical level by a materialism that leads to an obsession with money and consumer spending; to the scandal of EEC food mountains in a starving world; and to the utter failure of modern, secular society to discover a coherent *telos* of the Aristotelian kind and to its consequent aimlessness.[5]

The result is that the various injustices perpetrated 'mirror our own warring face,' for to change the kosmos we must first change ourselves; as John Fowles tells us, 'the dividing line between the Few and the Many must run through each individual.'[6] By now, the poem has well earned its final, typographically separate line, which offers a stark contrast to the multitude of evils that beset us: 'too little peace.' A verdict that may well stand as summation of Egan's political poetry as a whole.

3

Egan's first volume *Midland* (1972) contains a sequence of five brief lyrics entitled 'Poems For Northern Ireland' (CP 38-42) which chronicle, with ever increasing cogency, the tragic violence that exists in that divided community.

In the first poem of the sequence, 'November,' the protagonist is enjoying the sensuous nature of a mild autumn afternoon in Meath, before going home to tea. The detail of woods, grass, and river, of fish and rabbits, is nicely sketched, but what we are dealing with is, again, nature as moral metaphor, an idyllic world proceeding, as always, in its endless cycles and here uncontaminated by fallen man. But not quite idyllic and uncontaminated. The demise of the Big House and its way of life as symbolized by 'a lodge of musty ghosts' suggests that human life is subject to once-off, radical change, and the animal world as symbolized by the rabbits perceives man to be hostile (even if he is not), so that the theme of conflict, which brings about such changes, is introduced.

The poem closes with comment on that conflict as experienced in Northern Ireland. In order to contrast the violence there with the peace of Meath, Egan cleverly highlights its latent violence in the innocent world of nature.

So as we contemplate murder by its gun, human hearts are scattered instead of the leaves; 'the death-speck' replaces the 'patterning specks' of birds; the bullet swims instead of the fish; and in the evening, instead of there being 'such peace/as deepens on evening sounds,' life comes to a violent end.

If November anticipates winter and so death, spring suggests renewal of life and hope. In the second poem of this sequence, 'Palm,' Christ, invoked in the first poem, is seen as 'riding in triumph through Belfast' on Palm Sunday. The emphasis in this poem, uniquely among the five, is therefore on joy and hope, on the promise inherent in the message of Christ. For Northern Ireland is a place where people take their various strands of Christianity — Roman Catholic, Anglican, Non-Conformist, and others — seriously. But at the same time, the thrice repeated Aramaic word *Eloi*, meaning 'my God' and recalling Christ's words on the Cross: 'My God, my God, why have you forsaken me?' (Matthew 27:46; Mark 15:34), suggests that, for all the enthusiasms of Belfast's Christians, they, like the denizens of ancient Jerusalem, will go on to crucify Him. Which they proceed to do in the next three poems dealing respectively with a riot, arson, and a car bomb.

The third poem, 'Riot,' offers a striking example of Egan's early imagism. In nine lines of absolute asyndeton and remarkable economy, crucial details serve as a kind of metonymy for the theme of an intercommunal riot, in which a man is seriously injured and brought to hospital. Once more a basic opposition emerges between the world of nature and the violence of man, between the promise of life held out by the flowering of cherry blossom in the spring and the reality of what actually happens. But here nature too has been disrupted and mirrors, in an *abab* thematic scheme, what has been done to the man: the spray of cherry has been broken off and casually dropped in the hospital grounds, just as the man's life has been fractured and he is brought to the hospital; the pink and white colours of the cherry spray become the blood of the man and his pale, naked shoulder. But nature, though disrupted, is silent 'in strange stillness,' while the man's eyes, capable even in injury of speech, are seen as 'screaming.'

In the fourth poem, 'Fire,' the poet witnesses a fifty-year-old butcher's shop set on fire by arsonists on a Sunday. Far from Christ 'riding in triumph through Belfast' on Palm Sunday, escorted by women and children, we have instead the desecration of the Sabbath by the Antichrist of the dragon (*Revelation* 12: 1-17), as Christ's portrait 'handing above the mantlepiece' is consumed in the fire, caused by men. Sectarian men who take it upon themselves to execute this *auto-da-fe* (Portugese for 'act of faith'), originally the sentence of death passed on heretics by the Inquisition, and therefore usurp God's right over life and death in the name of one branch of Christianity.

So this local fire, which may well mean the end of the butcher's living, takes on a kosmic significance, as both the butcher and the poet wonder whether it can be put out in them by the water that came from Christ's side at the Crucifixion. If not, then we are faced with the destruction by fire recounted in *Revelation* (9:13-21), the Stoic *ekpurosis* at the end of the world.

The fifth poem, 'The Northern Ireland Question,' is privileged by its title, its position as the concluding poem of the sequence, and its status as independent poem in *Poems for Peace*. This 4-line poem, which possesses the clarity and power of the best Greek epigrams, is a striking *tour de force*:

> two *wee girls*
> were playing tig near a car . . .
>
> how many counties would you say
> are worth their scattered fingers?

The poem works through setting up a radical binary opposition between the children and the car bomb that obliterates them. On the one hand, the two young girls, neatly identified as Northern through the dialect '*wee girls*,' evoke the innocence of childhood with its easy companionship and devotion to play. On the other, the car bomb represents the fallen world of adulthood with its brutal antipathies and its appalling violence. This basic opposition can be formulated in other ways: the female world of the children is destroyed by the male world of violence; their personal integrity by the abstraction of 'counties'; their physical presence by the proxy bombers; so that their living, touching fingers are transformed into dead, untouching matter. Invited to contemplate this grim scenario, the reader can give only one answer to the rhetorical question posed: 'none.'

This theme of the violence exacted upon the people who live in Northern Ireland is continued in the poem 'Hitchhiker,' contained in the volume *Seeing Double* (1983) and also published in *Poems for Peace* (CP 190-91; PP 21-22). In style discursive rather than epigrammatic, 'Hitchhiker' finds the poet in the Irish Midlands giving a lift to a middle-aged Catholic man called Jim from Tyrone and so brought face to face with the Northern problem: 'The North was sitting beside me/outside Mullingar.' For we are presented with a catalogue of the horrors which have forced this man to leave home and become a refugee: his wife was killed in a Republican paramilitary bank raid at the age of 25; he lost his job with a Protestant firm because, after the perpetrators were caught and given life sentences, the boss was afraid of reprisals; and now — the last straw — his home has been destroyed: 'yesterday his cottage/bombed/and smoking up into the Dungannon sky'.

But the focus of the poem is on the *reactions* of Jim, his 'First Communion daughter,' and the poet to these events. These reactions are stoic in the extreme, for the price of violence here is not only its physical devastation of life, livelihood, and home, but its psychological devastation of people. Inured to violence and its aftermath, Jim is totally passive in his acceptance

73

of it — 'his voice softly accepted awful things it held/too much like the travelling bag' — so that he entertains 'no hard feelings' for the boss who lets him go and clearly envisages answering his own rhetorical question 'and what could anyone do now?' with the answer 'nothing.' His daughter, we learn, cried *only twice* in all of this, when her mother was killed and when she was sent to live with neighbors after the house was burnt.

But what about the aftermath of that death, what about the lost livelihood?

Accidentally confronted with this tragic story, the poet can offer passing, material help — the lift, dinner, some money — but is also numbed by the horror. So philosophical conclusions, corresponding to 'the politics of the last atrocity,' are not appropriate, nor, for that matter, is moralizing about the way working-class people like Jim behave in these situation. In the final analysis what impinges most upon the poet's psyche is not the violence itself, but rather the most vulnerable of the people affected — murdered wife, displaced child — and the pain they suffered. Pain is also felt by the man: he carries with him photographs of his wife and daughter, torn down from a wall where they had been fastened by adhesive tack.

'Hitchhiker' has a dual text, in which the main poem is flanked on the right-hand margin by a secondary poem with a shorter line, the latter having a variety of functions that include comparison and contrast. Here the secondary poem functions as contrast, because the character named Jack — suggesting the Taoiseach (Prime Minister) of the day, Jack Lynch — experiences, unlike Jim, a normal, peaceful life: not given to over-exertion, Jack is able to enjoy what must seem to Jim to be the luxury of a leisurely smoke of his pipe and discussion about hurling at a pleasant Sunday lunch with his friends; while Jim cries, Jack smiles.

The theme of Northern Ireland is continued in 'Hunger Striker' (CP 196), but the focus is broadened to include the complex relationship between England and Ireland. On record as believing in 'British determination to keep a hold on this island indefinitely,'[7] Egan chronicles what he sees as British colonialism in 'their dustbin empire' of Northern Ireland and British incomprehension of the Irish problem — as well as the apathy about Northern Ireland in the Republic.

Dealing with the IRA men who went on hunger strike in 1984, 10 of whom died, this unrepentedly nationalist poem begins with the total inability of English prison warders to understand why men would want to go on hunger strike for a principle, Irish men who are the modern counterparts of the millions who starved to death in the Famine of 1847, while Britain did nothing, men who are not ready to join in the banal rituals of a secular society such as queuing in supermarkets and washing the car on Sunday. At the end of the poem we see that this Englsih incomprehension is not confined to the working class, but extends to the highest levels of the Establishment in London, indeed to Margaret Thatcher, who appears at the end, grinning. The English colonial mentality is spectacularly indicated (as a note tells us) by the fact that 'English troops in a company in Aden were given a Robertson's jam label for every unruly native they shot': 'teeth grin like Robertson's golliwogs.'

In 'Hunger Striker' the secondary text, couched in a demotic British English, illustrates the banality of English working-class reaction to events in Ireland, a banality of the type that reaches mind-boggling proportions in the Tory-controlled sewer press. After various ritual remarks — 'top 'em,' 'terrorists I call 'em' — the six times repeated 'know wot I mean' is highly ironic, since what they say does not, precisely, constitute meaning, and the final phrase 'wot's yer poison?' shows that these people do not, in any case, take the issue seriously, since they are more interested in the next drink.

But the Republic of Ireland is not innocent either, for it has inevitably been corrupted by the process of colonization, so that the colonized mirror aspects of the colonizers, as Desmond Fennell's book *The State of the Nation* and Vincent Buckley's book *Memory Ireland* have so forcibly documented.[8] In the Republic, then, we have, above all, *apathy* which is violently denigrated at *Revelation* 3: 15-16 (used as an epigraph to Fennell's book) and so seen here as a form of death. This apathy about Northern Ireland corresponds to that of the prison warders in England, existing in the same banal world of quartz watches and ensuring that, even when there is a demonstration about Northern Ireland in Dublin, the participants go on, like the warders, to the cosy routine of 'a jar the tea.' At the same time, the Dublin Establishment and their warders, the Gardai, are just as involved in repression as the British and so travel 'the same road.' Independent Ireland is still deeply colonial in its attitudes.

These attitudes are explored at greater length in the volume *Siege!* (CP 99-112), which deals with the events that followed the kidnapping of Dutch industrialist Tiede Herrema by Eddie Gallagher and Marion Coyle, when they were besieged at a house in Monasterevin, Co. Kildare, for 16 days before finally surrendering to the police. More than any of the works so far examined, these seven poems deal with ambiguity and paradox. So while they do not possess the kind of thematic unity found in poems like 'Hitchhiker,' this is not necessarily a disadvantage, for Adorno warns us that 'a successful work is not one which resolves contradictions in a spurious harmony, but one which expresses the idea of harmony negatively by embodying the contradictions, pure and uncompromised, in its innermost structure.'[9]

The mode, then, of *Siege!* is that of *The Waste Land* of Eliot — who is indeed quoted in section IV — complete with epigraphs, an appendix, notes, and quotations from other languages (Irish, Greek, Latin, Italian), together with the added device of a photograph of the besieged house. The prevailing concept, however, is Platonic, the famous notion of human life as a cave — the Greek word for which is used in Section VII — from Book 7 of the *Republic* (514-521).

Given the dominance of this Platonic concept, the manifold imperfections of human life come as no surprise. Here they include a meretricious preoccupation with success, an even more meretricious obsession with making money — exemplifed in bizarre and spectacular fashion by Mr. E. Williams' contemporary and ungrammatical revision of the 1916 Proclamation: 'Irishmen and Irishwomen, in the name of God and (sic) future generations let us make a profit.' The utter irresponsibility of media hype heightens the poet's sense of outrage at the debasement of Irish nationalism both by paramilitary gunmen and by repressive overreaction on the part of the Irish State.

This overreaction is chronicled in sections I and II, which deal respectively with the Gardai and the Army. Significantly, the intense dragnet undertaken by the Gardai in order to find the kidnappers is compared to 'tenders of Blacks and Tans' and so to British repression in Ireland. Furthermore, the fact that the police come to raid some houses at night represents an inversion of human values, since the night should be given, not to violence and its aftermath, but to love, as the emphatic version of Ovid, *Amores* I. 13.38, in which the lover wants the night to last forever and so prevent the soldier taking arms (line 14), serves to indicate. In an equally evocative way, the Army marksman of section II is, though 'a shy quiet man,' equated with a military machine and, though Irish, with a British ranger.

As we move in section III to the kidnappers and their victim, what is stressed is the degrading nature of the whole enterprise, perceived by the imagination that penetrates the cave. On this melancholy scenario the quotations in Greek, Irish, and Italian pass ironic comment. Heraclitus' famous dictum that 'everything is in flux' not only draws attention to the contingent nature of the world of sense perception, but also links up with the Platonic cave, since Heraclitus' critique of sense perception helped to bring about Platonic dualism, the real world of the Forms, this world of the cave. Then the application to the three besieged people of the term 'lotus eaters' from *Odyssey* 9 serves to emphasize not only the unreality of the siege, for it must end, but also contrasts the way the kidnappers are engaged in violence with the peaceful nature of the Homeric lotus eaters. Similarly, the quotation in Irish from the song *Róisín Dubh*, in which Spanish wine is promised to Róisín, that is to Ireland, mocks the Ireland that no longer looks to Spain, but to England, as the journalists drink in a pub with the unimaginative English-type name, 'The Blue Helmet' (which also suggests a bobby's helmet) and play the English game of darts. Finally, the quotation from Dante (Sonnet 1 of *Vita Nuova*) dealing with the light coming from stars, when the personified figure of Love appeared to the poet, serves to stress the darkness of the cave (as with the line from Sophocles' *Philoctetes*) and the Discord found there.

And yet things are never that simple. For the imagination, no matter how penetrating it may be, cannot, with justice, fully understand and delimit any human being.

The title of section IV, 'Fugue,' suggests that we will be dealing with antithesis and so indeed it proves. As in other poems, nature, here viewed in the context of the European pastoral tradition, functions as moral metaphor for normal, peaceful life. But as the poet picks 'the last wood mushroms' of autumn, the world of the cave and its violence suddenly intrudes chillingly upon his namesake: 'the evening/ Sergeant Egan/ got his finger/ blown off.'

Section V deals with the debasement of Irish nationalism by people engaged in a violent raid upon a bank — itself far from innocent, since it is a central part of a materialistic culture (cf. CP 214) — to get money to cause more violence. So when the men attack the bank's porter, the quotation from Dante (Sonnet 24 of *Vita Nuova*) once more offers ironic comment on what is happening: the thoughtful men on a religious pilgrimage contrast with the mindless men who rob a bank, and Italian has to be brought, brutally, up to date, so that the phrase *in petto*, 'on the chest,' refers to the robbers attacking the porter. Consequently, the question addressed to Ireland in Irish must be revised, so that it means 'where, in all of this, is the Ireland genuine revolutionaries fought for?'

Egan presents further ironic comment in section VI, which deals with the end of the siege and focuses particularly on the media hype.

In the world of the cave nothing, of course, is what it seems. Independent Ireland has to import experts in sieges from the former colonial power, Britain, now given to materialism ('Why pay more?'). The media jamboree is so excessive in its manipulation of participants and the audience that it represents the sort of military repression that Britain and others engage in ('like Nato troops'), mirrors that of the Irish forces of 'Law and Order,' and so constitutes the antithesis of what Father Prendergast, hanged in this very place after the 1798 rebellion against Britain and commemorated by a monument standing in a silent square, stood for: 'Unity, Courage, Freedom.' All three of the leading actors are 'prisoners,' since Eddie Gallagher and Marion Coyle go to jail, he being heavily sedated and she kept in solitary confinement for four months, and since Dr. Herrema goes to holiday in the

Bahamas, where he will not escape himself. And, finally, all of this has taken place in a state itself given, like Britain, to materialism; for when the whole thing is over, the only constant in the world of flux is 'the lorries of commerce rolling up and down the Naas road.'

But the final section (VII) makes it clear that the poet is not a detached, innocent observer. Lured by the publicity, by a sort of voyeuristic curiosity, for which he twice asks pardon like a penitent confessing sins (*'mea culpa'*), he makes his way to the scene of the siege through the conflicting images of the Irish Midlands: their beauty (evoked in a phrase from a celebrated Irish poem), their role in the Celtic myth of Fionn (whose Fenian encampment was sited on the [visible] Hill of Allen), their invasion by modern materialism in the form of machines, — the firm Roadstone indeed dug through the Hill of Allen — neon lights, banal architecture, inadequate facilities for recreation. But this *ersatz* modern pilgrimage is, of course, to no avail, for the house is now just like any other with 'no sign of *anything*,' inhabited merely by ghosts. Ghosts created by the media, of even less account than trivial modern film, and no match for the pagan Fionn or the Christian Brigid from nearby Kildare. The world of the cave, indeed.

Two other poems — 'Young Gifted — and Unemployed' (SF 11-12) and 'Breaking' (CP 214) — provide cogent comment on the reality of life in the Republic of Ireland today. Opening the volume *A Song For My Father* and so programatically establishing the theme of exploitation that is central to the first part of the volume, 'People,' the poem 'Young Gifted — and Unemployed' deals with the scandal of massive unemployment in contemporary Ireland.

For most of the poem the main text chronicles the monotony and futility of the daily life of those who cannot find work and must live on the dole, while the sub-text bleakly underlines this by constantly repeating the key words 'job' (8 times), 'loss' (4 times) and 'dole' (3 times). Those who tolerate this appalling situation are the comfortable middle class who are devoted to sentimental *ersatz* country music and whose message to the young is 'Pissoff Pissoff.' But there is also another strand of response in the poem, that of the spirited resistance of the young unemployed people to the situation, and it is on that note of insouciance that the poem ends:

jooooooooooooooooooooooobb

but never you mind! the mornings'ours

sssssssssssssssssssssecuuurrr
secsecsecsecsecsecsecsecc

we'll swing into in a gear gang

ah morning morning

young young young one last time

of a day that

and sometimes unemployment's another high

turned

out

on which we float and don't give a damn

different

about adults waiting with the washup

    The Republic is also in question in the poem 'Breaking,' addressed 'To the Directors, Bank of Ireland Finance.' The topic is economics, but economics is, properly, a branch of politics — as the Greeks and Romans well knew and as Egan, well versed in Pound, might be expected to hold with. In the poem the physical breaking of a horse by stable boys near the poet's home functions as a symbol of how human beings are psychologically broken by the exorbitant interest rates charged by banks, whose only aim is to make profit. It is worth recalling in this context that in 1986 the Irish Government paid in interest to Irish banks, the sum of IR£541 million, that is the people of Ireland paid this large amount — roughly equivalent to the cutbacks in state services proposed by the Government in 1987-88 — to the private shareholders of these banks.

    So it is entirely appropriate that Egan's sub-text here includes the word 'usury' five times and the word 'slavery' twice, quotes the commercial bastardization of the proclamation of Independence already referred to — 'Irishmen and Irish women in the name of God and future generations let us make a profit' — and ends with 'interest/interest.'

4

The next four poems to be considered here embrace the large themes of nuclear destruction, prefigured in the dropping of the atomic bomb on Hiroshima; of the United States and the Soviet Union as superpowers; and of the division of Germany. They demonstrate a tendency in Egan's poetry away from the personal towards the universal, from Ireland towards the world at large, from a private towards a public tone. As he himself has said in a lecture on 'Poetry and Commitment,' 'the older I grow the more engaged I seem to get.'[10]

    If the poems as a group have the nightmare of recent contemporary history as a general theme, 'Ground Zero' (CP 192; PP 15) addresses itself to the future. Faced with the prospect of a so-called 'limited' nuclear war in Europe, the poet, as European, appeals to all Americans 'who have not grown old' to ensure that this catastrophic scenario be never enacted. The United States derives from Europe, both physically in terms of ethnic composition and spiritually in its appropriation of the ideals of the Roman Republic and of the French Revolution — So those Americans who preserve the ideals of the Founding Fathers and who therefore continue to offer the world a message of hope are asked to 'save Europe.' This includes Russia with its Indo-European language and great literature, then oppressed by a totalitarian system.

If the Americans act with vision, they will remain true to their great heritage and will follow the injunction to 'save your present selves.' Above all, they will be saving the ordinary people who live in Europe, like the inhabitants of County Kildare with their 'lovely midland sky.' (Again nature and the human beings who inhabit its landscape function as paradigm for normal human life.)

The horrific alternative of nuclear war is vividly realized in powerful language. A hydrogen bomb would explode with 'inhuman mushrooming heat' and bring human life to an end, so that we could encounter the paradox that the kosmos as we experience it is totally destroyed because of man's endless capacity for knowledge, that it may become 'radioactive with pride.'

As we move from potential nuclear war to the actual dropping of an atomic bomb on Hiroshima, the brief poem 'Hiroshima' provides us with the raison d'être for 'Ground Zero.' This poem deals with the catastrophic impact of this — so far — unique event at three levels: those of history in general, of the individual people directly affected, and of the poet as commentator.

In terms of history, the cataclysm of Hiroshima is such that even its shadow has, paradoxically, the power to 'burn into' history, conceived of as the hardest stone, granite. The normal selectional rules governing the verb 'burn,' which require it to have a subject capable of performing this action, are broken, so that what seems an ineffectual, insubstantial thing like a 'shadow' does have, because of the enormity of Hiroshima, this power over history. (At the same time, we think of the shadow of a woman burnt into granite steps when the bomb exploded.) By a similarly paradoxical way this mere shadow also ensures that those who journey to Hiroshima as pilgrims, like the poet, are afforded 'a wide serious space/where one may weep in silence.'

But the crux of the matter is, of course, the incredible capacity for destruction possessed by nuclear weapons: 'one hundred thousand souls/ fused at an instant.' And, as in the sequence 'Poems for Northern Ireland,' the most vulnerable victim is a child. A child who is, literally, 'burnt' and so represents at the level of the individual person what has already been said about history in general, a child who cannot speak and so constitutes an exemplar for the silent pilgrim.

But there is, nevertheless, some hope. The burnt child is offered a cup of water by a soldier 'tenderly,' so that not all military men are of the type who have wreaked this destruction. And Hiroshima has so impinged upon the psyche of the international community that, in homage to the burnt child, children from all over the world have left paper birds at the Children's Monument as symbols of hope: 'the delicate paper cranes.'

The poems 'Germany' (CP 194-95); PP 25-26) and 'Learning Russian' (SF 23-24) present two contrasting ways of looking at international politics. In 'Germany' art is set aside to concentrate on politics, on the division of Germany after World War II; in 'Learning Russian' the reverse process takes place and Soviet imperialsim is set aside to concentrate on art, on the great Russian writers, filmmakers and musicians.

In 'Germany' we have again a priamel, in which the foil puts aside the topics of German composers like Schubert (though the secondary text, which presents a Schubert song, shows us what would be involved), poets like Heine, novelists like Broch, and painters of the calibre of Altdorfer, Lovis Corinth, and Nolde. What the poet wants to talk about, the climax, is the Berlin Wall, at that time symbol *par excellence* of the division of Germany into West and East. Happily, this is no longer the case — but 'Germany' still holds its weight as a commentary on the psychological effects of partition anywhere. The wall's paraphernalia of repression stand for the traumatic effect of division upon Germany: 'iron stays through your soul.' As Egan says in prose:

One principal holds for just about every country in the world: that which has geographical, cultural and (in the long term) historical unity must not be partitioned. Doing so guarantees permanent trouble.

This brings us back to Ireland, partitioned since 1922 and divided along community lines for hundreds of years, with the appalling consequences that we have already seen, summed up in the concluding lines of 'Germany': 'seven hundred years the sadder for it and/nothing to offer except a car bomb.'

In 'Learning Russian' the poet acknowledges that, when he was eager for knowledge 'in the hungry years,' when his sensibility was being formed, the serious part of his soul was indelibly impressed with the music, film, and literature of Russia, and so he was, in some sense, 'learning Russian.' Egan's vision here is, then, akin to that of Solzhenitsyn,[12] who is mentioned in the catalogue of honor: Russia is an essence, with a spiritual people, not circumscribed by the particular accidents of contemporary politics or by the failed imperialism of the Soviet Union.

Akin also to George Thompson's view of the Blasket Islands in Ireland,[13] this epic vision looks to a Russia whose spirit can be exemplified in its image of hospitable peasants prior to collective farms and industrialization, of a beautiful, but formidable landscape and climate, and of the artists who have given such eloquent testimony to both people and country. These themes, and not politics, are what nourish the poet; if 'Germany' deals with the limitations of art, 'Learning Russian' does so with the limitations of politics.

5

Before coming to Egan's poem about specific parts of the Third World, a more general poem 'Feed the World' (SF 48) should be examined. Just as the section of *A Song For My Father* called 'People' begins with the theme of exploitation, with massive unemployment among the young in the developed world, so the section closes with a poem about the starving millions of the Third World. Addressed to Irishman, Bob Geldof, the organizer of that remarkable event *Live Aid*, the poem not only endorses his Herculean efforts to bring immediate hope to the famine-stricken people of Ethiopia, but proposes, more radically, that the phenomenon created has almost succeeded in uniting the disparate parts of the world into some brief wholeness:

> — for the first time since Cain did the dirt
> you come the nearest I know to gathering the world
> however briefly back into one

For Geldof could hardly have reckoned with the enormous impact of his project: at the literal level, he has brought food to the starving and can therefore be compared to Christ who fed the multitude (Mark 6:30-66; John 6: 1-15); at a symbolic level, he has reminded the First and Second Worlds that they too once experienced famine — as Ireland did in the 1840's — and still experience such social evils as unemployment; most crucial of all, Geldof, like Christ, has brought a world starved of metaphysical nourishment to realize that 'Man shall not live on bread alone' (Matthew 4:4, Luke 4:1):

> how could you guess how far your
> loaves and fishes would go?
> or that you would help us rediscover
> something lost down memory?
> break our apartheids?
>
> and as no one lives on bread alone
> feed us who are also starving?

6

Egan's poems about Chile, the Falklands, the Philippines and South Africa
are characterized by two central motifs: firstly, the struggle of the people
against viciously corrupt and repressive regimes, whether the right-wing
dictatorships of Pinochet in Chile and Marcos in the Philippines, the racist
apartheid rulers of South Africa, or the imperialist government of Thatcher
in Britain; secondly, the use of Ireland, itself long oppressed by British
colonialism, but eventually to gain its freedom, as paradigm, as evidence
that in the end the struggle of the people will be successful.

So in 'Brother Sister Chile' (SF 36-37) the Chileans, imprisoned and
tortured under Pinochet, are invited to allow Irish men and women to speak
on their behalf:

> they have gagged your voice
> take ours instead we
> will speak for you will cry
> across the world at your agony

Such Irish solidarity, which derives its force from Ireland's centuries of
struggle against colonialism and recent achievement of independence ('both
old and young'), is ultimately spiritual and so beyond the reach of the
military. Three images suggest its power: images of voice, light, sky. The
solidarity is such that its verbal articulation in 'the deep/ undying anthem of
freedom' will penetrate, as ongoing echo, into the silent, curfewed streets;
that its light will illumine the darkness of the prison Chile has become; that
it constitutes, at a time of despair, the hope of a patch of blue in the sky.

If Chile is oppressed by its own, the Malvinas or Falkland Islands are
oppressed by British imperialism: the British recapture of the Falkland
Islands in its 1983 'war' must be seen as a last fling of Empire, undertaken
to satisfy British chauvinism, and as Egan says, 'a reminder that political
expediency can outweigh all logic, expense, morality and sense of the
ridiculous.'[14] The witty poem 'H.M.S. Fishfingers: The Falklands' (not yet
published) appropriates the powerful sonnet 'Ozymandias' by Shelley, an
Englishman who supported Ireland's cause, to make a comparison between
Margaret Thatcher, who presided over this late imperial venture, and Ozymandias, who saw himself as 'king of kings.' Just as Ozymandias regarded
his achievements with great pride, as the secondary text from Shelley makes
clear — 'Look on my works/ ye mighty/ and/ despair' — so too does
Thatcher. But Ozymandias came to nothing and the verdict of history on
Thatcher's imperialism will be similar:

like bottles of port
a few khaki shells   *Look on my works*
stamped *Empire made*   *ye mighty*
                                            and
whistled like rubber bullets
across the Pacific   *despair*
at 12 British knots per decade

buried themselves
in its warm malvine sand
another agreement

for exhibition
to tourists of the past

with the genitals of Ozymandias

   In time to come, those who wish to discover the past will discover, not in the
Falklands, but in the Malvinas, the military shells that are the debris of Empire,
shells ironically seen, in a parody of the jingoistic slogan 'send in a gun boat,'
as slowed down to '12 British knots per decade,' after being fired from H.M.S.
Fishfingers. These curiosities, equated with 'the genitals of Ozymandias' —
wasn't the whole thing a balls? Isn't Thatcher a bollocks? — lie buried in 'the
warm malvine sand' and so remind us, like Shelley's closing verses, of the
wreck of Empire: 'Round the decay/of that colossal wreck, boundless and
bare,/the lone and level sands stretch far away.'
   With the poems 'For Father Romano On His 45th Birthday' (SF 32-33, PP
23-24) and 'For Benjamin Moloise' (SF 16-17, PP 13-14), we move from the
general effect of political repression upon a country to its particular effect
upon the individual person who challenges that repression.
   The poem about Father Romano, also issued in poster form by Amnesty,
pays tribute to him as a representative of those priests and lay people who try
to bring a better way of life to its disorganized, exploited poor in the remote
villages of the Third World, to the people Fanon calls 'wretched of the earth.'[15]
Very often this work for the poor is seen as subversive by a corrupt Establishment and repression ensues: Father Romano disappeared, presumably ab-
ducted by Government troops (he has not been seen since; on a visit to the
Philippines, Egan was told by a journalist that Romano had been tortured and
then dumped from a helicopter into Manila Bay).
   Since Ireland has contributed to this struggle through its many missionar-
ies in the Third World and since Romano himself spent a year in Ireland, he
too can count on Irish solidarity in the form of the poet's potent mixture of rage
at what has happened and pride in those who take a stand for justice, at the risk

of their lives.

A pride all the more cogent because Romano's spirit will prevail over any military repression. The suffering priest is perceived as a type of Christ, who, if killed, will rise again from the dead, for 'the resurrection continues.' Consequently, Romano will always have a community of followers to celebrate his life and the gates of Hell, the evil of repressive dictatorships, will not prevail against him and his like, as they march not like troops before saluting officers, but towards truth and justice and brotherhood: 'no one can stop our march.'

It is not far from the Philippines to South Africa and the repression of the racist *apartheid* system, in which the white colonial government oppresses the black community *because they are black*. So in the poem 'For Benjamin Moloise,' who was executed by hanging in Pretoria in 1985, the solidarity felt by the people of the world with Moloise demands assimilation to his color — 'when they hanged you we all became black' — and condemnation of the authorities who try 'to dangle Africa from a white noose.'

Moloise, then, stands for freedom for the black people in South Africa and his courage in fighting for that freedom contrasts with white repression in the shape of teargas and the *sjambok*, the whip made of native rhinoceros or hippopotamus hide, but given an alien Afrikaans name and a racist purpose of beating black Africans. Moloise's death is, in one sense, a defeat, but the silent mourning of the world is eloquent testimony against white South Africa with its gold and affluent suburbs; the quicklime that destroys his body cannot destroy his spirit. This notion is extended to suggest that Moloise's spirit, though he was killed in the night, represents a new dawn for Africa and the world, as the poem's final line 'Benjamin son of days' serves to emphasize, since in Hebrew the name Benjamin means not only 'son of the right hand' (i.e. *auspicious*) and 'son of the south,' but also 'son of light/day'.

7

Egan's political poetry is characterized by commitment, by a considerable range of theme and treatment, and by defamiliarizing language. An achievement all the more remarkable, because on the one hand he himself has written a great deal of very fine private poetry and because on the other Irish poets (Yeats excepted) have not written much political poetry at all and tend in that poetry to confine themselves to the Irish question, and, in general, to avoid commitment. Certainly, Egan is the most *engagé* of contemporary Irish poets.

Egan's commitment is truly human in that it acknowledges, in an altogether too infrequent combination, both society at large and the individual person. This means that he attacks the various repressive forces in the world, conceived of in a broad way to include both capitalist and communist systems, imperialism, a debased nationalsm, and the rampant materialistic consumerism of Western society. It is a measure of how totally the Enlightenment philosophy has failed to deliver[16] that the prevailing tone in all of this must be negative: Utopia, by etymology and definition, does not exist and no thinking person can feel that it is even remotely in sight. And the chilling portrait of both West and East in Saul Bellow's great novel *The Dean's December* serves to underline Egan's viewpoint.[17]

Commitment, by itself, is not, of course, sufficient; the literary treatment is what is crucial. Particularly striking in Egan's political poetry in the range of treatment: imagist, epigrammatic, and discursive poems about Northern Ireland; the emphasis on ambiguity and paradox in modern Ireland; the collage of other languages, in the extremely impressive sequence *Siege!*; the prophetic and angry tone of the Third World poems; the pathos of 'Hiroshima'; the wit of the Falklands poem.

This range is matched by quality of achievement — as the analysis advanced in this chapter is intended to demonstrate. This quality derives, essentially, from a combination of *vision* and the ability to articulate that vision in contemporary idiom.

In today's world political vision is all too often lacking and it is extremely refreshing to come upon somebody who is not afraid to offer a radical critique of the way we are, without sinking into the banal role of a *laudator temporis acti*. And while Egan does not offer a fully explicit programme of how things should be, the implicit programme is clear: freedom for states from outside interference; freedom for the individual person from repression by the State; a proper role in human life for things spiritual and a consequent rejection of materialism, at both a philosophical and everyday level; and the exaltation of love, directed towards both the individual person and society.

SEVEN

Thucydides and Lough Owel: The Greek Connection

1

In his essay 'Thucydides and Lough Owel: The Greek Influence' (SPr 113-27) Egan echoes Shelley's assessment of our debt to the Greeks:[1]

We are all Greeks. In the basic vocabulary of our thinking; in philosophy and in politics; in science, medicine, architecture, literature, in the very language we use and in our whole perception of the universe, we have been shaped by the Greeks. (SPr 113)

This general influence applies to Egan himself:

I have always felt a special affinity with things Greek, with the literature and the language, the art, myths and general mystique. (SPr 113)

What qualities, then, are involved here? First, Egan, following Simone Weil, chooses 'that accent of simplicity which is the stamp of Greek genius' (SPr 113). As exemplified, for example, in Callimachus' famous epigram on the death of Nikoteles, for which Egan rightly claims a 'shocking directness' and which is given here in his own translation:

> He was twelve, the child whom his father Philip
> Put away here and all his hope, Nikoteles. (SPr 114)

Which brings us to the second quality Egan sees in the Greeks, a 'clear-eyed truthfulness' (SPr 116), a refusal to offer easy answers or facile consolations. So Hector tells his wife Andromache in 'a most affecting passage' (SPr 116) that 'I know well in my heart and soul that the day will come when sacred Ilium will be destroyed along with Priam and the race of Priam of the good ash spear,' and goes on to speculate the Andromache will become a slave of the Greeks. Again, Hector's infant son Astyanax becomes frightened at the sight of his father's armour, with the result that, as Egan well puts it (SPr 116), we have 'Brutal realities faced-up to without flinching and make more poignant in the light of a peaceful world of family and friends.' For all the darkness depicted in Greek literature there is another, third

87

quality present which ensures that we are far from mere pessimism: human nobility. As exemplified in Sophocles' play *Philoctetes* when Philoctetes faces up to the fact that he must leave his island very much against his will and take part in the fall of Troy. A fourth quality arises out of the other three: a combination of 'passion and control' (SPr 64) which, running from Homer to the contemporary poet Ritsos, seems very Greek and involves both an intense commitment to human life and a detached observance of it.

To express these qualities the Greek had a great, subtle language. As Louis MacNeice puts it:

You find there are things you can do in Greek you never could do in English. The two negatives for instance — *ou* and *mé* — and even more the exquisite subtlety of the double negative *me ou*. And the wealth of particles. And that wonderful Greek word *an* which you can even tack on to a participle, so that where in English you would say 'Those who would have done this,' in Greek you can get rid of the wretched relative, say 'Those *an* having done this,' but 'having done' itself would be one word and not two.[2]

Egan would surely agree and adds some points of his own about 'the most expressive of all the languages of the West':

English needs an auxiliary verb to express the Passive Voice; lacks a Middle one — as it does the Optative Mood; makes little use of the Subjunctive. Nor has English anything like the range of nuance which Greek prefixes make possible — as they also do the effortless formation of compound words. I count in my Liddell and Scott lexicon no fewer than 58 double-column pages devoted to words prefixed by *epi* — from *epabelteroo* ('to make a greater ass out of') to *epokhros* ('yellowish'). (SPr 122-23).

2

The landscape of Egan's poems analyzed in Chapter Three is that of the Irish Midlands, though he hankers after the sea at times (CP 85-86); but there are a handful of poems that deal with the Mediterranean landscape of Greece and Italy — 'Crete,' 'Kazantzakis' house in Hiraklion,' 'Kybisteter,' 'Sicily' — and one — 'Thucydides and Lough Owel' — which connects Greece with the Irish Midlands.

Much of the undoubted force of the poem 'Crete' (CP 31-32) derives from a complex interaction of past and present. In Part 1 we have on the one hand the ancient Minoan civilization of Crete, which began about 2,500 B.C., and came to an abrupt and violent end about 1450 B.C., when Crete was hit by a tidal wave after a cataclysmic volcanic eruption on the island of Thera (modern Santorini); we have on the other hand the modern island with its tourists and mechanized ships. Equally well, there is continuity: in 'the groves of the ancient cicadas'; in the climate and ever-present sea; in the age-old rituals of farmers and peasants; in the ruins left by the past.

Minoan civilization is not easy to come to grips with some 3,500 years later: the glazed earthenware of Minoan art — like that from the temple at Knossos, the Minoan capital — is distant; the light of day is radically different in its brightness from that of Northern Europe; the Minoan world can only be approached imaginatively through the proverbially impenetrable labyrinths of Knossos:

> remote
> brown faience
> challenging
>
> lights honeyed vertigo
>   reality
>   spinning
> (memory's Knossos
> the rustling labyrinths)
> as in the nebula of a dream

In contrast, there is a vignette of a contemporary farmer who is very accessible indeed with his 'leather leggins breeches harsh face.' At the close of part 1 of the poem, these two versions of the island — Crete remote, Crete accessible — are brought together: the poet does arrive there safely, brought by the modern ship, but he is conscious too of the distant past when Crete, close to Africa, engaged in large-scale commerce by 'the fertile waves.'

In part 2 of the poem we have moved to Phaistos, a town which stands on a hill at the west end of the Mesara plain in southern Crete, 3 1/2 miles from the sea. Designated by a travel poster as 'the new place,' Phaistos was a large town that boasted an elaborate palace in the Middle Minoan period (1700-1550 B.C.). So here again ancient and modern coexist in symbiosis: on the one hand a peasant is beating an octopus (Greek *khtapodi*) on the rocks to soften it for cooking and a waitress is serving retsina to thirsty tourists; on the other, we can see the vivid, naturalistic frescoes of the Middle Minoan period (even if they and the walls on which they are painted are in ruins), the gold drinking cups of Minoan art, and, as an analogue for the modern waitress, 'the shy wasp-waisted' goddess of Minoan religion. There is therefore both contrast and comparison between ancient and modern, but the poem ends by emphatically stressing the ancient: as darkness descends at night from Africa — southern Crete had close links with Egypt — what we are left with is the remnants of Minoan civilization, salvaged from the tidal wave that destroyed it:

> the only emperor
>
> African darkness
> *frescoes littered through masonry*
> *golden cups in the muddy trees*

Another poem about Crete, 'Kazantzakis' house in Hiraklion' (CP 52), deals with the decaying house of the great Cretan writer Nikos Kazantzakis, author of novels such as *Zorba the Greek* and *The Last Temptation of Christ*, and also of a substantial modern poem on the theme of Odysseus:

> high windows railings brass knockers
> surround its gap
> in the thin mouth of the street
>
> wallpaper
> flitters against the rubble

The mood of this concentrated five-line poem is obviously elegiac as the house is now in ruins, but, since this is one of those texts which achieves its meaning through what it does not say,[3] we must probe further. While the poem's closing, poignant image of disintegration deals with Kazantzakis' house, what we are to infer is that, for all of his literary efforts, Kazantzakis the man must, like everyone else, like Shelley's Ozymandias, die. The poem is therefore both an elegy for Kazantzakis, and a meditation on the contrast between what we try to do (and partly do) and what finally awaits us all. The 'thin mouth' hints at the way Cretans rejected Kazantzakis—some even spat on his grave in Hiraklion.

A third poem about Crete, 'Kybisteter' (SPr 126), deals with a piece of visual art and we recall Egan's assertion that Greek sculpture is 'usually the first thing I head for in a museum or gallery' (SPr 125). The piece is a small ivory figure of a *kybisteter*, an acrobat vaulting over a bull, which dates from about 1500 B.C. in the Middle Minoan period and is now in the archaeological museum in Hiraklion:

> a slender form
> floats in air
>
> wards off with ivory arm
> cold horns
>   the earth's field
>   the deluge of space

Cretan
poise
one long moment's freedom

later
the irrelevant fall

As Egan points out, this figure 'represents for the first time the free movement of a body in space' and so anticipates some of Degas' work in this area by 3,500 years (SPr 125). The poem therefore concentrates on the specific moment of vaulting, when the acrobat 'floats in air,' avoiding not only the bull (this statuette has not survived), but also the earth and all the rest of space. So what the acrobat achieves in this position is poise and freedom, a triumph that mirrors those of Minoan Crete in general, before its civilization was destroyed.

3

And yonder in the gymnasts' garden thrives
The self-sown self-begotten shape that gives
Athenian intellect its mastery . . . .[4]

Yeats's verdict on the astonishing, the unique achievements of 5th century Athens, in which he asserts that they derived from a Platonic Form on earth, is endorsed by Egan in his essay on the Greeks. Egan refers to a number of Athenian achievements — Sophocles' *Philoctetes*, Euripides' *Medea*, Plato, Homer, Callimachus, Athenian sculpture — but the work he likes best is the *History of the Peloponnesian War*, the conflict between Athens and Sparta that lasted from 431 to 404 B.C., by Thucydides; indeed he goes so far as to declare that the *History* is 'probably my favorite prose work' (SPr 117).

Why, then, this preoccupation with Thucydides? Because for Egan Thucydides exemplifies *par excellence* the qualities described in section 1 of this chapter: an austere simplicity, a full confrontation with the reality of war, a keen awareness of the nobility of Athens, and, not least, an incredible restraint. Furthermore, there is striking originality, because Thucydides invented the dramatic speech put into the mouth of a character and aimed at giving us the essence of a particular situation and of the character's personality. Such as the famous Funeral Speech of Pericles in praise of Athens in Book 2. Or Egan's choice above the others, Nikias' speech in Book 7 before the final battle of Syracuse in 413 B.C., which brought to a disastrous end the Athenian expedition to Sicily. Here is a part of that speech:

Soldiers of the Athenians and of the allies, the conflict before us will be exactly the same for all, and each one of us, just as much as the enemy, will be fighting for his life and country; for if we achieve victory now with our ships, each man can again see his native city, wherever it is. But we must not lose heart or behave like very inexperienced men, who, if they lose the first battles, ensure that the expectation engendered by their fear does not rise above their misfortunes. But those of you here who are Athenians, already experienced in many wars, and those who are allies, constantly fighting by our side, must remember the unpredictable element in wars and must get ready to do battle again in the hope that fortune will be with us, and be prepared to fight in a way worthy of this great army of yours, which you see before you.[5]

For Egan, Thucydides' restraint, 'his ability to get out of the way of what is happening even as he re-enacts it in his account' (SPr 118), is central; he cites a classic example from Thucydides' description of the Plague that hit Athens at the beginning of the War:

I shall describe (the plague), having suffered it myself and having seen others who did.

Resisting any attempt to wallow in self-pity or even to give us full details of his case history, Thucydides tells us he had the Plague too in a mere half-sentence. Passion and control with a vengeance!

But Egan has not been content to write in prose about Thucydides, for we have a marvellous, very beautiful early poem called 'Thucydides and Lough Owel' (CP 30), whose title, as we have seen, suggests a programme for Egan's poetry, both parochial and international:

teal
    poised on ice
        above the lake's throb

this blue translucence
flexing across rocks

        frozen sprays of fern

— remind me of your History
for if the stretched town is become
part of nature   so
are your sentences

like gulls they cry
down the cold shores

In this imagist poem the season is winter, the month November, the setting Lough Owel in the Irish Midlands near Mullingar. Winter has frozen the lake and the vegetation; nevertheless, there is an extraordinary feeling of vitality behind all of this, exemplified by the blue teal which is poised, easily seen, ready for movement, and the lake which, although frozen, possesses a 'throb.' So we are back again to that mixture of control and passion, as the poised bird and frozen lake mirror the coolly passionate sentences of Thucydides that are readily intelligible. Just as the town of Mullingar is a presence like the phenomena of nature, so those Greek sentences of Thucydides have become part of what is normally available to us and make their claim upon us, as the birds of that natural world cry in the cold of winter. The style of this experimental poem is incredibly succinct, so that it suggests the style of Thucydides, itself a masterpiece of compression. A poem, then, that provides a truly remarkable distillation of the Greek spirit.

Another poem which features Thucydides is the richest of the poems about the Greco-Roman landscape, 'Sicily Sicily' (SF 28-29), written some 15 years later in the colloquial, though very concentrated, manner of late Egan. Here we meet again that curious combination of ancient and modern found in 'Crete,' and it is Greek Sicily — which dates from the extensive colonization of the island by the Greeks in the 8th and 7th centuries B.C. — that is finally more real for Egan: the beginning of the poem sees the poet trying to recapture his visit to Sicily like a Greek watchout on Mount Eryx (where Aphrodite had a temple) looking for Carthaginian ships coming from Libya during the several centuries in which Carthage colonized the western part of the island; part of the centre of the poem is devoted to Thucydides' account of the Athenian expedition to Sicily — although, inevitably, the present obtrudes, so that we find the traveller literally reading 'Thucydides in a traffic jam'; and the end of the poem has the poet reminding himself of the island by imaginatively carrying a coin of Greek Sicily in his wallet. Again, the poem refers to the town of Selinus on the west coast, which was founded by the Megarians in the 7th century and flourished in the 5th century, when its many Doric temples were built: 'the Doric skyline of Selin-unte.'

The central image of Greek Sicily in the poem derives from Thucydides' account in Book 7 of the collapse of the Athenian expedition and, in particular, the final naval battle in the harbor of the Corinthian colony of Syracuse in 413 B.C., a conflict described by Egan with graphic power:

> that vast bay of Siracusa beyond imagination
> coldblue murderous
> where the triremes had thumped and smashed and

>   drowned slowly like men
>   dragging down the Athenian dream partly our own
>   to break the surface again in history's flotsam
>   with Nikias' last speech

This was a catastrophic defeat for Athens from which she never fully recovered and, since Athenian civilization in the 5th century has had such an enormous impact upon Europe right up to the present time, the sinking triremes affect us as well as Athens. But as Louis MacNeice puts it, 'Though Athenians died, Athens no longer dies,'[6] so that out of the wreckage of ships and empire Thucydides has constructed a powerful tragedy which has lasted down the centuries and is epitomized for Egan in the last speech of the Athenian commander Nikias, who exhorted his men:

Stand firm now if ever, remembering, each one of you going on board, that you are the fleet and army of your country and all there remains of the city and of the great name of Athens.

Indeed the impact of the Greek past is so intense for the poet that he hears the babble of contemporary tourists in Syracuse 'turning Greek' and metamorphosed into the terrible cries of Athenian prisoners incarcerated in open stone quarries, afflicted by extremes of heat and cold, and each given, over a period of eight months, less than half a pint of water and less than a pint of food, so that, as Thucydides says, 'corpses were heaped on one another':

>   thousands of soldier sailors moaning dying
>   in limestone mines too hot then too cold
>   where caverns dripped despair and beneath overhangs
>   the shadows were *corpses heaped on one another*

Contemporary Sicily too has its black side: the sea is inexorable, the heat is still a killer ('the shirt sticking to my back'), the streets of Palermo witness on a daily basis murders by the Mafia: 'tyres screeching down the black mafia streets.' But ultimately how the poet will remember Sicily is by its marvellous Greek coins which constitute a symbol of its Greekness (and which Yeats used as the basis for the first coinage of the Irish Free State).[7] Specifically, for a silver coin of four drachmas from Syracuse, signed by the great innovative artist Euainetos[8] and portraying dolphins jumping out of the water around the head of the sea nymph Arethusa (who was transformed into a fountain in Ortygia, an island in the harbor of Syracuse, where she was united with her lover Alpheus).

In the final analysis therefore what the poem stresses is not the dark, but the bright side of the sea; not the Syracusans' brutal treatment of the

Athenians, but their art; not the hate of the Peloponnesian War, but the love of Arethusa and Alpheus; not, in short, the negative, but the positive side of the Greeks.

4

Another area of Athenian achievement that preoccupies Egan is that of tragedy, in particular the *Philoctetes* of Sophocles and the *Medea* of Euripides. He has in fact already translated *Medea* into English and has worked from time to time on *Philoctetes*, which he hopes to finish in the near future.

Rewriting Pater so that 'art aspires towards essence, towards simplicity,' Egan finds in *Philoctetes* 'the simplest of plots,' the attempt of Odysseus to get back Herakles' bow from Philoctetes because it is necessary to end the Trojan War in favour of the Greeks. Exemplary conciseness too — because in a mere 1471 lines Sophocles 'contrives to explore the most profound issues touching on human life' (SPr 120). As when Philoctetes realizes that Neoptolemos has betrayed him, that he has lost the bow, and that he must leave his island to help the Greeks, who abandoned him on it ten years before, to capture Troy; at that point Philoctetes has nothing left and no one to talk to but the island (Egan's translation):

> O harbors, O rocks, O haunts
> of the wild animals, jagged cliffs
> I'm talking to you who are always around
> because I have no one else. I'm weeping at
> what this youngster from Achilles has done on me.

For Egan *Medea* has a 'distilled quality' similar to *Philoctetes* in its treatment of the man/woman conflict and he rightly regards Medea as 'the first feminist heroine' (SPr 121). Egan's translation of Euripides' play succeeds admirably in capturing this feminism, which is worth exploring further.

Medea, who is the grand-daughter of the Sun-god and skilled in poisons, comes from Colchis and there helps Jason to acquire the Golden Fleece. They fall in love, get married, return to Greece, and have two children. But as the play begins, Jason abandons Medea in order to marry Glauke, daughter of the king of Corinth (where they live) and so provide himself with the security of marriage into a Greek royal family; as the Nurse says, literally, Jason 'sleeps with a royal marriage.' It is vital to understand that Jason enters into this new marriage, not for love of Glauke, but because she represents the security he craves. This is no eternal triangle in the modern sense; in fact it constitutes the reverse for *Jason loved Medea, but just wants to be married to Glauke*.

We can develop further the binary oppositions inherent in this intensely dramatic situation. Beneath the umbrella of the man/woman conflict there are the added polarities of custom (*nomos*) versus nature (*physis*); of city (*polis*) versus house (*oikos*); of marriage (*gamos*) versus sexual love (*eros*); of Greek versus foreigner. In other words, Jason stands for the public world of the Greek city and its value-system, which stresses marriage, Medea for the private world of the foreign person and her value-system, which stresses love.

As a foreigner, Medea is in a special position to demolish Jason's system and that is what she proceeds to do with devastating effect. For Medea not only engineers the death of Glauke and Glauke's father, King Creon, but also, horrifically, kills her own two children, *and is then given sanctuary in Athens by King Aegeus, brought there from Corinth in the chariot of the Sun-god*. So this quadruple murderess is endorsed by the gods and the city of Athens — surely one of the most shocking statements ever made in the history of Athenian drama; something to send shivers down every male back during this intensely civic occasion in the Theatre of Dionysus, the god of paradox; the reason, surely, Euripides came only third in the contest in 431 B.C. But also, as we can now see, the tragedy is the first major feminist statement in European literature and one of the greatest: Medea is a great woman, driven to excess by love and man's selfishness.

The first test of any translation of a play must be its capacity to capture the essence of the original's story-line, and Egan has certainly succeeded in doing that with *Medea*: the man/woman conflict is splendidly caught. One reason for Egan's success is that he avoids the twin traps that constitute the Scylla and Charybdis of all translators: on the one hand, translation which, by giving the letter, obscures and ruins the spirit of the original; on the other, translation which is more a version, executed by a translator intent upon obtruding him/herself into the original.

What we have here — and it is a rare phenomenon — is the genuine article, a translation that sticks rigorously to the original, but not in a way that presents ludicrous language of the type parodied by Housman. Indeed, Egan would pass the test suggested by another accomplished translator from the Greek, Richmond Lattimore:

[The translator] must use all his talents, his understanding of the language and of the meaning of the original and his own skill in verse, to make a new piece of verse-work which represents, to him, what the original would be, might be, or ought to be, must be, in English. This will be neither the original-in-English only, nor the author-helped-by-original only, but a product rather than a sum of the two.'

Two particular aspects of Egan's considerable achievement should be noted. First, register of language. Egan sticks at all times to an emphatic modern register that avoids both archaism and neologism, and is therefore a pleasure to read. Consider, for example, this extract from one of Medea's speeches attacking Jason (which preserves the sibilance of the original in lines 2 and 3):

> I'll begin at the very beginning.
> I saved your skin (as those Greeks know
> who sailed with you on the *Argo*)
> when you where sent to yoke-up the fire-breathing bulls
> and sow the deadly field with dragon's teeth.
> I also killed the serpent who coiled around the Golden Fleece
> never sleeping, guarding it with his twisted coils,
> and I raised for you the light of deliverance.
> Then I betrayed my own father and my home
> and went off with you to Iocos under Mount Pelion,
> a woman more eager than wise.
> I killed Pelias in the most painful of ways —
> at the hands of his own children. I finished the whole house.
> And having got all this out of me, lowest of the low!
> you betrayed me, found yourself a new bed
> after our children were born.

Second, the choral odes. Here Egan scores a remarkable success by keeping in these notoriously tricky passages (very difficult in Greek, never mind English) to his emphatic modern register and rigorously avoiding any lapse into translatorese. Consider, for example, the Chorus' praise of Athens:

> The Athenians, sons of Erechtheus, have been blest from of old;
> offspring of the blessed gods, sprung from a sacred, unconquered land,
> finding their nourishment in
> supreme Wisdom always moving gracefully
> through the luminous air. There, once upon a time,
> they say the Nine Pierian Muses, the pure ones
> gave birth to golden Harmony. . .
>
> How then could this city of sacred rivers,
> this land that provides
> safe escort for friends, receive you,
> murderess of her children, an impious woman, among her other citizens?
> Think about the shock to your offspring.
> Think about murder and all it destroys . . .
> Do not, on our knees we implore you
> by everything, by everyone —
> do not kill your children!

Egan's *Medea* is, then, one of the most successful translations of this era and gives the lie to Virginia Woolf's belief that 'It is useless to read Greek in translations: translators can but offer us a vague equivalent.'[10] As Egan himself has said, poetry 'consists of that essence which *can* be translated' (SPr 40). And here *is*.

EIGHT

Landscape Into History

1

EGAN'S tenth collection of poems, *Peninsula*, deals with the Dingle Peninsula in west Kerry in the south-west of Ireland. County Kerry constitutes part of the uplands of the South of Ireland, 'the post-Carboniferous east-west Armorican folds, consisting of ribs of old Red sandstone flanked by Carboniferous Limestone.'[1] These ribs form steep-sided promontories, of which the Dingle Peninsula is one.[2] The limestone has   provided durable construction stone for megaliths, field walls, farmsteads, and churches.

The pattern of habitation in the peninsula was that of isolated farmsteads rather than of the villages that characterized England and much of Western Europe. The inhabitants eked out a precarious living through farming and fishing, and their culture had a marked oral character.

Peninsula consists of 34 poems: 27 deal with various aspects of the Dingle Peninsula, 6 with the massacre at Dún an Óir (Smerwick), and the volume begins with the Epilogue.

The central themes of the 27 poems that come first in *Peninsula* include: a concentration on place — the title of virtually every poem is a place name; a feeling for history that makes the Dingle Peninsula at once old, new and eternal; a view that the area is very special, indeed unique. These themes are presented in poems of great brevity: only two ('The Great Blasket 1969' and 'Minard Castle') are over 20 lines; as many as 19 consist of 10 lines or under; 4 have a mere 5 lines. This brevity makes for a remarkable, epigrammatic conciseness and a power that is further enhanced by the pervasive asyndeton (less than 20 occurrences of 'and' in the 27 poems). The mode, then, brings to mind Egan's earlier style, as exemplified in the 1972 volume *Midland*.

That the Dingle Peninsula is unique is often suggested in these poems. Kerry, which is best appreciated by the mature, needs nothing added to its ancient landscape, since it is as distinct as Sicily and since it is, crucially:

> . . . sustained by its own truth

This truth is not accidental, but is produced by the way of life of the Kerry people and especially of the fisherman who grapple with the Atlantic, all described as:

> this necessity

What, then, is involved in Kerry's necessary truth? First of all, unity: the landscape at Ballynagall — 'mountain cloud the wine sea' — seems to bring about a return to some primeval unity:

and everything becomes one again

With this unity comes an unbroken, unfractured state exemplified by the romanesque art of the 12th century church at Kilmalkedar:

this wholeness

It is a wholeness demonstrated by the unique landscape of Kilfountan that makes for faith in God and an art which matches that faith with a:

has a feel to it a
souterrain quickening
some wholeness all its own

one of those places where
belief might earth itself

and ogham and cross converge
in one graceful pillar

Equally special are the Kerry people. At an everyday level, the farmer in 'Tourists' exhibits 'that delightful/Kerry delay' and we encounter the phenomenon of 'that/puzzling Kerry handshake.' At a fundamental level the people are:

... a people who hope for little
forget nothing and
make no easy act of faith

They are also fiercely independent, like the two brothers fishing in that special currach of the south-west, the *naomhóg*, who are:

where no one can reach them

Language is of course central to human beings and the Irish language is central to Kerry people, as the poem 'Wardsmaid in Dingle Hospital' makes clear. The Irish of the Kerry Gaeltacht exhibits an 'extraordinary power and beauty,'[3] here demonstrated by the authentic accent of the wardsmaid that recalls the noble Gaelic past. Her use of Irish is such that it not only reenforces the idea that the *logos* — meaning, as in Heraclitus, 'the true account

of the law of the universe'⁴ — is present in Kerry — 'its own truth'; 'this
necessity'; 'this wholeness' — but also suggests the Incarnation of Christ as
logos (a Christ who himself spoke Aramaic):

> and her response comes in a swell
> and the old Gaelic kingdom is there
> in a *blas* never lost to schooling
>
> and the word is made flesh

The uniqueness of the Dingle Peninsula is not only a matter of language —
Irish is still spoken freely in parts — it is closely bound up with its landscape
and its history.

Egan's poems capture all those facets with deft strokes reminiscent of a
painter: the local Irish place names; the ever present sea of many moods with
its 'atlantic light,' 'its ocean smell,' its mackerel, lobsters and gannets; the
mountains, cliffs, valleys, rain; flowers such as fuchsia, honeysuckle, bog
cotton; fine examples of early Christian art. As in the exemplary poem
'Ballynagall Strand':

> light is ebbing and
> its failing pathway
> gilt silver
> leads wet sand out towards the
> mystery of the bay
>
> and everything becomes
>
> one
> again

The last line shows the extraordinary power of this landscape, a supernatu-
ral quality referred to again in 'holy Mount Brandon' and Gallarus, 'a sacred
place.' Indeed nature in the shape of a mountain near Anascaul can seem: an
intimation

This landscape can appear truly idyllic:

> I would drive more than 200 miles
> for such a breakfast

And yet a landscape that is so much a part of daily living that it is 'unnoticeable.'
We move on to history — but even here Kerry cannot be confined: it seems

to exist before and out of history; the Dingle Peninsula constitutes 'these eternities'; Kerry experiences 'some *continuum*'; the mountains called The Three Sisters belong 'out of prehistory'; the bog cotton at Feohanagh 'trembles there out of time.' Indeed such is the timeless quality of Kerry that in 1,000 years time the waves at Ballydavid strand will sound:

> as if for the first time

When we do come to something that is definitely of a period — the oratory at Gallarus that may date from the eighth century* — its impact is such that is appears modern after more than a thousand years:

> light from the eighth century still
> splays from the east into our gloom

Similarly, in Corca Dhuibhne the writing in Old Irish (ogham) is eternal, reflecting a perpetual element in human beings:

> such undeciphered ogham
> forever on whatever people are

Why these examples of ancient Irish art can still be so riveting is indicated at the end of 'Gallarus': they derive from nothing less than a Platonic Form to produce a combination of great faith, great artefact, great artist that has been irrevocably lost in the modern secular world:

> its wholeness moulded
> along Platonic lines drawn out of stone
> when it and the fingers the hope cohered
> watertight

We come to more recent history in 'Ballyferriter,' that of Piaras Feiritéar, the last of the 17th century Irish leaders to hold out against the English, who was hanged publicly in Killarney in 1653, but whose poetry lives on particularly among Irish speakers in the Dingle Gaeltacht.[5] Here the mood is profoundly elegiac, as the Irish spoken in Ballyferriter — 'the town of Feiritear' — masks the collapse of Gaelic civilization, becomes a mere veneer over the reality of historical loss, loss initiated with the massacre of Dún an Óir and with the execution of Feiritéar:

> that old wonderful resistance   *has it been pining*
> *since Sybil and Piaras died*
> *and the 600 at Dún an Óir*

The more overtly historical 'Minard Castle' continues this theme of Gaelic loss. Minard Castle at Kilmurry was the last of the Fitzgerald castles to be built on the Dingle Peninsula — probably about 1550 — and was blown up by Cromwellian forces about 1650. Though in very poor condition the castle still stands and, like so much else in the Peninsula, possesses an authority, an 'energy,' that demands attention. This energy derives from its tragic history which continues to project itself, some 350 years onwards, into the present, just as the mass murder of Drogheda's citizens by what Yeats calls 'Cromwell's murderous crew'; with the result that we may experience

> a whisper from ancestors
> like those whose Drogheda skulls
> were unearthed recently clubbed-in?

This elegiac note is found also in the poem 'The Great Blasket 1969' which eulogizes the ancient heroic lifestyle of the subsistence farmers and fishermen of the Great Blasket Island off the Kerry coast, compared by George Thompson to that recounted in the Homeric poems. This heroism found its fitting chroniclers in the works of Peig Sayers (*Peig*), Muiris O Súilleabháin (*Twenty Years A'Growing*) and, in particular, the masterpiece of Tomás O'Criomhthain, *An t-Oiléanach* or *The Islandman*.[6] This great work

recreates a climate made up of a profound acceptance of the realities of life coupled with an intense appreciation of the mere physical joy of living reduced to its simplest terms.[7]

Or as Egan puts it:

> ...mediocrity
> never became the norm out here
> where existence is an exile

This lifestyle remained unchanged for centuries, but the inexorable advance of what we are pleased to call progress brought about the removal in 1953 of the last of those living on the Great Blasket; as O'Criomhthain foresaw when he wrote:

ná beidh ar leithéidi arís ann ('our likes will not be there again').[8]

For Egan the abandonment of the Great Blasket is one more nail in the coffin of Gaelic civilization:

dear dear place
empty in the last mild collapse
of a once-great Gaelic vision
which persisted into our time

2

So far in *Peninsula* history has indeed been felt, even commented on, but, with the exception of 'Minard Castle,' only indirectly. With the Dún an Óir sequence of six poems, however, we come to a more explicit treatment, involving three other languages — Irish, Italian, and Spanish — as well as English, of the central issue of Irish history since the Norman invasion of the 12th century, that of English colonization, here presented in a lengthy account of a particularly brutal massacre of the Irish and their continental allies by the English at Smerwick Harbor in County Kerry in 1580.

The historical background is, briefly, as follows.[9] From the beginning of Elizabeth's reign in 1558, there was constant friction between the English colonists and the dispossessed native Irish. In 1570 Pope Pius V absolved the Irish from allegiance to England and recognized King Philip of Spain as king of Ireland. In 1578 Pope Gregory XIII sanctioned a Papal expeditionary force. Two years later a force of some 600 Spaniards and Italians with 6,000 muskets landed at Smerwick in Kerry to join an uprising of the Irish led by the Earl of Desmond.

This force was besieged by the English in Dún an Óir fort (the name means Fort of Gold, probably referring to pyrites in the rock) in the winter of 1580.[10] The Irish, Spaniards, and Italians surrendered after being offered quarter by the Deputy of Ireland, Lord Grey, who commanded the English (Bingham was another commander). But Grey then instructed Walter Raleigh and his men to massacre everyone — men, women, children — sparing only the treacherous leader San Giuseppe and a few of his cronies. Some were hanged; three, including a Father Moore, were tortured; virtually all died. The verdict of Cyril Falls on this massacre may be regarded as definitive:

Many more terrible acts have been committed in war, but the cold horror of this has continued to leave its mark upon the pages of history after over three centuries and a half.[11]

Among those present at the massacre was the poet Edmund Spenser, secretary to Grey, who denied in his work *A View of the Present State of Ireland* that quarter had been offered to the Irish and their allies.[12] Spenser is supported by his editor Renwick,[13] but the noted Irish historian Alfred

O'Rahilly[14] has shown decisively that quarter was offered and that the Italian leader Sebastiano di San Giuseppe betrayed his men. O'Rahilly's summary is masterly:

It is so hard for Spenser's editor to believe that the poet should combine with Grey and the Italian to hide the infamy which saved Ireland for the Empire. But for us it is no harder than believing in the butchery of men and women by 'the good Lord Grey,' the Artegal of the *Faerie Queen*, and by Raleigh 'the summer's nightingale' to whom it was dedicated.[15]

In the Dún an Óir sequence the movement towards discursive history is beautifully gradual: the first poem (I) consists of a mere 8 lines, 29 words with no main verb, in total asyndeton; the Spanish forces and language are not directly mentioned, but subtly alluded to by the nautical terms 'pinnaces' and 'galleon,' which derive from Spanish *pinaza* and *galéon*; the backing of Pope Gregory XIII for the Irish, though more overt, is still muted in the phrase 'papal ensign'; the Irish themselves remain 'silent'; and, not least, the powerful zeugma

> watching from cliffs
> from centuries

encapsulates in a single allusive word, which brilliantly ends the poem, the long English domination of Ireland.

We begin our entry proper to discursive history in poem II: the poem has over 30 lines; Italian and Spanish are quoted directly; the Irish, far from being silent, are 'crying,' 'screeching,' 'pleading'; the poem at one point turns completely paratactic with five successive occurrences of 'and'; and English domination is all too obvious.

This English domination goes far beyond the mere suppression of the Irish and their allies: directed at Dún an Óir against unarmed men, women and children — who, in the words of Bingham himself, were 'very ragged and a great part boys'[16] — it is viciously violent, brutally barbaric:

> and already the ropes are out
> and already the swords are swishing
> and steel thrusts into the screams
> and hammers thud from the forge
> where they brought Father Moore

This gratuitous violence involves an implicit, but emphatic comparison between Elizabethan civilization and Elizabethan barbarism. In the Elizabethan period Italian influence upon English literature was marked: Wyatt and

Surrey wrote sonnets about love in the Italian mode of Petrarch; Sir Philip Sidney, son of the Deputy for Ireland and a defender of his father's government of Ireland to Elizabeth, not only succumbed to this fashion, but also received the Queen's leave to travel and learn foreign languages; Spenser, present at Dún an Óir, used Ariosto and Tasso as models for *The Faerie Queen.*

Futhermore, the Elizabethans produced great translations from other languages: in 1561 Hoby's translation of Castiglione's *The Courtier*; in 1567 Golding's *Metamorphoses* from the Latin of Ovid; in 1579, a year before Dún an Óir, North's *Lives of the Greeks and Romans* from the Greek of Plutarch (mediated through the French of Amyot); in 1581, a year after Dún an Óir, the famous *Tenne Tragedies* from the Latin of Seneca.

But at Dún an Óir the English find unintelligible the pleading of the surrendered in Spanish and Italian; just behind culture lies barbarism:

> under no flag
> their weapons surrendered the surrounded
> *very ragged and a great part boys*
> reason in the wrong languages
> *por favor por favor per favore*
> discovering their despair

A point graphically underlined by the quotation from Raleigh, the perpetrator of the massacre:[17] for all his commitment to poetry — 'The Passionate Man's Pilgrimage' has been described as 'a great poem'[18] — his knowledge of Castiglione's *The Courtier*, and his realization of human pain, Raleigh has presided over this barbaric slaughter. Pleased to mock Aristotle,[19] he is blissfully unaware of one of Aristotle's central insights into the human condition: 'Intellect alone moves nothing.'[20] Raleigh intellectually grants to 'cruel Time' — Horace's *fugaces anni* — the ability to bring about death, but has not the *will power* to prevent himself from arbitrarily anticipating Time by killing people:

> weasel eyed Raleigh leads a young girl
> back to the fold
> *Oh cruel Time, which takes in trust*
> *Our youth, our joys, and all we have*
> the looting and drinking is almost done
> and drunken anger closing-in

Still less do the other English leaders — Grey, Bingham, Zouche — qualify in reality as Tudor humanists: the massacre does not impinge upon them at all; as might be expected given Grey's view of the Irish as 'this scum'

and 'this detestable crew,'[21] and Bingham's refusal in Connacht to observe
the usual rules of law for the Irish.[22] These Elizabethan adventurers are, then,
deluded: the founding of Trinity College, Dublin in 1592 does not expiate the
massacre at Dún an Óir and Yeats' verdict (in his great sonnet 'Meru') on
what passes for civilization is more than apt:

> Civilization is hooped together, brought
> Under a rule, under the semblance of peace
> By manifold illusion ....

The burden of poem III of the sequence is that history is not located in the
distant past, but is alive in the present, 400 years on:

> you can feel it still
> the desolation

Those present are on one hand the Spaniards, Italians, and Irish, on the
other, the perpetrators of the massacre, Grey, Raleigh and Elizabeth herself.
Egan graphically recounts the fate of those slaughtered, while simultane-
ously and sardonically attacking English perfidy: '*Grey's faith and
Raleigh's mercy*.' The poem ends with a powerful passage that begins with
Elizabeth's praise of Grey for the massacre,[23] relentlessly chronicles the
murder and torture, and then once more brilliantly contrasts English culture
with English barbarism, creating a conceit typical of Elizabethan poetry, so
that Phoebus, the sun god Apollo, becomes present at the slaughter:

> *a gloss on this late enterprise performed by you*
> *so greatly to Our liking*
>
> after the few women had been raped
> one more time and decapitated like chickens
> after the last head tossed to the cove
> and body unroped heeled out
> after the final child sworded-through
> the sledgehammers dropped did
> Raleigh and Macworth escort Grey
> to inspect the remains of the agreement and
> did they advert to the wintry beauty as Phoebus
> hid his wat'ry lock beyond the
> shoals of corpses?
>
> in the crying of these fields

In poem IV of the sequence the tone drastically changes. The massacre is no less real, indeed its awful cost in human suffering is brought before us 400 years on with a vividness and power unmatched in Irish poetry since late Yeats. But the human nobility of the Irish, Italians, and Spaniards; their ardent belief in God, Catholicism and the Pope; the use of their three languages — Irish, Italian, Spanish — which swamp the mere 5 lines of English in the poem; the complex interaction of the two texts which pile up the testimony; the quotation of a 17th century Irish poem by Fear Dorcha O Mealláin that, unlike Raleigh's, is in total harmony with the rest of Egan's poem (note the religious sentiment in both) — all this contrives to suggest that it is the despised foreigners and not the English who emerge triumphant from this ghastly confrontation. The English then and now do not understand Ireland, do not understand Irish, are notoriously unable to speak foreign languages, enjoy now a secular society, indulged in a late imperial venture as recently as 1982 (the Falklands War). It is in that total context that we listen to these wretched of the earth:

dove è San Guiseppe?
che cosa face
ho studiato a Firenze
mi padre! mi madre!
perchè perchè perchè?

go tapaidh a Mháire bhig
síos leat ar an gcosán san
le taobh na h-aille
sar a dtagann siad thar n-ais
ag lorg níos mó díghe
slán agus beannacht a mhúirnín
go tapaidh! cloisim arís iad
ag iompar na gcorpán

The climax of the sequence comes in poem IV; with poem V we revert to a more measured tone which contrasts in a devastating way with what has gone before, partly because the English language has reasserted itself, a linguistic fact that mirrors the military fact. Here once more there is an implicit comparison between English barbarism and English culture: how can Spenser devote himself to a 'most careful and beautiful Italian hand'[24] (the main text), how can he write an emphatic eulogy of the Countess of Pembroke, sister of Sir Philip Sidney, supporter of Elizabeth's policy in Ireland (the sub-text),[25] when he has witnessed, condoned, approved of the massacre? The answer of course is that the winners in history, blind to their own defects, attribute them to the losers, proceed inexorably with the acquisition of Empire, themselves chronicle, in their own interest, what has happened.

As we bear in mind that Sir Thomas Smith, one of Elizabethan England's leading intellectuals, who held that England was superior to all other nations, asserted that the English were the new Romans come to civilize the Irish,[26] an apposite commentary on the Dún an Óir massacre can be found in the words of the Scottish leader Calgacus, who castigates the Romans in Tacitus' *Agricola* (30): [27]

Brigands of the world, when no more lands exist for their indiscriminate plunder, they now attack the sea. If an enemy is wealthy, they are greedy; if poor, they lust for power; and neither East nor West has satiated them. Alone among mankind they desire countries with resources and countries without resources with an equal passion. Robbery, butchery, rapine they call, using a false name, Empire and, where they create desolation, they call it peace.

The last poem of the sequence partly reverts in its form to that of the first — as there we have brevity, 11 lines, 47 words, and asyndeton — but now we have a succession of main verbs which comment graphically on what has happened and Irish has replaced Spanish, in part the tortured Irish of poem IV, in part that of local placenames. The mood here is extremely sombre — key words include 'death,' 'blood,' 'horror' — the 'hope' of poem I is now gone. What has transpired is that the massacre and all its horrors have become part of nature, inseparable from the elements of land, air and water: there is 'blood on the grass,' air that suggests a hanging body, 'death stinks from the bay.' Indeed such is the fusion of massacre with nature that the elements and the birds cannot cleanse the area of what has happened. Finally, the cliffs have become animate and speak, naturally, in Irish, language shouted by Irish men and women at the time of the slaughter:

> *éist éist*
> the cliff screams at Árd na Ceartan.

It is ever the mode of the powerful — as Barthes[28] and others have so cogently shown — to make their way of doing things appear natural, the norm, the only possible way; as here Grey, Spenser, and the rest of the English. But in this concluding poem nature refuses to accept that position and instead endorses the defeated Irish.

3

In *Peninsula* Egan has moved on from the sense of place in *Midland* and *Athlone?* and the sense of history in *Siege!* to a striking combination of landscape and the past. In regard to both of these entities he is more emphatic than previously: *Peninsula* contains a very clear-cut view of the Dingle Peninsula and dispenses with the question-mark accorded *Athlone?* The Dún an Óir massacre, while providing room for the contrast between civilization and barbarism outlined, does not deal with the ambiguity that is at the heart of *Siege!* The reasons for this are at least two: firstly, Egan has possesses a new authority since the volumes *Seeing Double* and *A Song For My Father*, an authority applied to both locality and political history; secondly, Egan can apply this authority to the Dingle Peninsula — as he cannot in the same way to the Midlands — because he has substituted for the arrogance of President Kennedy's 'Ich bin ein Berliner' the humility of:

> I am an outsider

If that sense of being an outsider is found also in the Epilogue, as the poet is seen working in his Kildare study, if the quotation from the Portuguese poet Pessoa hints with ironic self-depreciation at the struggle to write, so too does this further Romance language recall the Spanish and Italian of the Dún an Óir sequence, so too does the remembering of Kerry lead once more to a simultaneous realization of its landscape, its eternal aspect, its tragic history, qualities of the Dingle Peninsula that, because truly part of the human condition, affect everyone:

> landscape of tragic presences
> where time fades to eternity
>
> that great grey movement
> over us all

Desmond Egan: An Annotated Bibliography
COMPILED BY BRIAN ARKINS

I. Works By Desmond Egan

A. Poetry

1. *Midland*. Goldsmith Press: Newbridge 1972. With drawing by Brian Bourke. This introspective and imagist volume deals mainly with the theme of the Irish Midlands, but the landscape in Egan is 'more radically transforming than anything in Ledwidge or Kavanagh' (Connolly, no. 58, 103). Furthermore, the splendid poem 'Thucydides and Lough Owel' shows that Egan is to be both local *and* international, while the sequence 'Poems for Northern Ireland' anticipates the major role that political themes will play in Egan's later poetry.

2. *Leaves*. Goldsmith Press: Newbridge 1974. With drawing by Charles Cullen. As Egan has said (no. 54, 22), 'Where *Midland* is landscape, *Leaves* is figures in a landscape and maybe one figure in particular.' This special figure is a woman and *Leaves* chronicles her relationship in a series of very successful love poems. Of particular note are two poems that memorably recount the end of the affair: the title poem 'Leaves' in the discursive manner of late Egan and the brief 'Requiem' in a very effective epigrammatic vein.

3. *Siege!* Goldsmith Press: Newbridge 1976. With photograph by courtesy of Pat Maxwell Agency. Though brief, the volume *Siege!*, which deals with a famous, politically motivated kidnapping in the Republic of Ireland, is a watershed in Egan's poetry. Here he adopts with great success 'an essentially Eliotic technique' (Connolly, no. 58, 104), which also owes much to Ezra Pound. It involves the use of epigraphs, an appendix, notes, and quotations from other languages (Irish, Greek, Latin, Italian) to comment in Modernist form ironically on the debasement of Irish nationalism and on the lowering of public standards in our times.

4. *Woodcutter*. Goldsmith Press: Newbridge 1978. With photography of sculpture by Albert Giacometti. This volume partly features the Irish Midlands, which are captured with a marvellous concise elegance. *Woodcutter* also encompasses a wide thematic range greater than heretofore: a man dying of cancer; love poems which include the haunting and accomplished 'V —'; a splendid defence of 'this rural stuff' in 'Not on the course'; and a poignant, powerful elegy for Ezra Pound, which has become quite famous.

5. *Athlone?* Goldsmith Press: Newbridge 1980. With photograph by Fergus Bourke and map by Sir William Petty. Here Egan moves from the landscape of the Midlands to a characteristic small town, Athlone, where he grew up. With low-key treatment already guaranteed by the question mark that follows the title poem 'Athlone?,' this sequence of 22 poems lovingly portrays the minute particulars of everyday life in a

small Irish town, so that this body of authentic details comes to constitute what Egan elsewhere calls '*the real thing the sacred / mood*' (no. 8, 216).

6. *Snapdragon*. Appeared in no. 8; U.S.A. 1992. With drawing by Brian Bourke. This volume consists of a series of 12 love poems and lends weight to van de Kamp's view that 'Like Yeats, Egan writes books rather than individual poems' (no. 64, 3). As always in Egan, the possibility of loss is present, but so too is happiness, and what distinguishes this love poetry is its maturity in allowing for both sorrow and joy. This complexity is underlined by Egan's refusal to give any title to 10 of the 12 poems: he uses the first line as title (a device associated with Marianne Moore and further underlining Egan's readiness to exploit Modernist experiment).

7. *Seeing Double*. Goldsmith Press: Newbridge 1983. Illustration by Alex Sadkowsky. A richly satisfying volume, *Seeing Double* establishes beyond doubt that Egan is a major poet, whose literary programme rejects symbolism and insists on the concrete splendor of life. The thematic range is very impressive: elegies for Irish poets Watters and Ledwidge; political poems on Ireland, Germany and America, and on the deprived people of the world; the need for philosophy. A major technical innovation is the use of a dual text, where the main poem is flanked by another on the right-hand side which 'functions very flexibly in different instances as parallel or counterpoint, as parody or homage to the main poem' (Connolly, no. 58, 105).

8. *Collected Poems*. National Poetry Foundation: Orono 1983; 2nd edition, Goldsmith Press: Newbridge 1984. This volume, which won for Egan the National Poetry Foundation of America Award for 1983, contains the volumes just described, nos. 1-7, with a new 'Introduction' poem and prose introduction — the latter dropped from the second edition. The achievement here is major and makes the neglect of Egan in various anthologies of Irish poetry incomprehensible. Those who really understand poetry know better, such as Hugh Kenner who said in launching the *Collected Poems* (in Washington, D.C., 1983): 'With Desmond Egan we come to a poet who is hospitable in a new way to the literary traditions of Europe and America — in a way no English poet is.' Another way of describing Egan's work here is to say that he has finally married the local intensity of Kavanagh with the knowledge of Yeats.

9. *Poems for Peace*. Afri: Dublin 1986. With an introduction by Sean MacBride and drawing by James McKenna. Includes, with some new material, 'The Northern Ireland Question' from no. 1; 'Ground Zero,' 'Hitchhiker,' and 'Germany' from no. 7; and 'For Benjamin Moloise,' 'Brother Sister Chile,' 'For Fr. Romano on his 45th Birthday,' and 'Peace' from no. 10. This short volume emphasizes the increasingly political nature of Egan's poetry and his willingness to tackle major international issues. These poems are characterized by a deep sense of the injustice that pervades the world and by a commitment to peace in the case of both society at large and of the individual person.

10. *A Song For My Father*. The Kavanagh Press: Newbridge/Peterloo Poets: Calstock 1989. This volume is divided into two sections: I: People and II: Sequence: A Song For My Father. The content of section I underlines once more Egan's local and international allegiance with: poems about Midlanders such as the great tenor John McCormack and Oliver Goldsmith, and about international figures from South African freedom fighter Benjamin Moloise to Fr. Romano of the Philippines. Again,

Egan's social concern is emphasized by the programmatic positioning of the poems 'Young Gifted — and Unemployed' and 'Feed the World' as the first and last poems in the People section. Section II consists of an elaborate elegy in 18 poems for the poet's father, in which Egan meditates brilliantly on three forms of reality: the eternal everyday, death, and love.

11. *Peninsula*, Poems of the Dingle Peninsula. The Kavanagh Press: Newbridge 1992. With photographs by Liam Lyons. From chronicling the landscape of the Irish Midlands (see esp. nos. 1 and 5), Egan here moves on to meditate on the Dingle Peninsula in Kerry. Central to his view of this breathtaking area is the conviction that landscape is a wholly necessary, but unobtrusive part of human existence: 'the/ unnoticeable landscape.' Consequently, the majority of these poems are brief, employing — as in *Midland* (no. 1) — the mode of imagism to capture a moment of present time in its minute particularity. But in the Dún an Óir sequence which concludes *Peninsula*, history and the more discursive mode proper to it enter in, as Egan castigates the massacre by the English in 1580 of 600 Irish, Spaniards, and Italians, whose plight is emphasized by the use of the Irish, Spanish, and Italian languages in section IV.

12. *Euripides—Medea*. Translated by Desmond Egan, with an introduction by Brian Arkins. St. Andrews Press U.S.A./Kavanagh Press Ireland 1991. Egan is on record as believing that '*it is possible to translate*' (Arkins no. 55, 120) and has very successfully demonstrated the truth of his dictum in this new translation from the Greek. For Egan's *Medea* splendidly captures the man/woman conflict of the original; sticks at all times to an emphatic modern register of language that avoids both archaism and neologism; and is very accomplished in his translation of the notoriously tricky choral odes. (This important translation was staged in a readers theater production in Omaha in February 1991 and was presented in four performances in Little Rock in October 1991.)

13. *Choice*. An anthology of Irish poetry selected by the poets themselves with a comment on their choice. Edited by Desmond Egan and Michael Hartnett. Goldsmith Press: Newbridge, first edition 1973, second edition 1979. Contains a favourite poem chosen by each of 53 poets and remains as fair and representative an Anthology of contemporary Irish poetry as there is.

14. *Poiemata, Readings in Poetry and Prose for Young People*. Chosen by Desmond Egan and Gerard Rice. Fallons, Dublin 1972. An anthology for young readers beginning English in Secondary Schools. A landmark in Irish School publications, not only by reason for the excellence of its content but also for its variety (from Su Tung P'O to John Berryman), its use of translation (from Greek, French, Spanish, Russian, Irish), and not least for a lively visual presentation which included photography, the cinema-still, drawing, painting and cartoon. All of this reflects Egan's own range of interests. It is notable, also, that the editors considered that only the best writing (and visuals) was suitable for youngsters: the Anthology is a very challenging one; it has been very influential.

15. Cassette: *Desmond Egan: Poet's Choice*. Selected from nos. 1-7, 9 and 10. Kavanagh Cassettes: Ireland 1989.

15b. *Selected Poems:* Creighton University Press: Omaha 1992. Selected and with an Introduction by Hugh Kenner. A superb selection of Egan's best work to date, including *Peninsula*.

B. Prose

16. *Focus*. With Eugene Watters. Fallons: Dublin 1972. Analysis of 50 poems; 24 by Egan, ranging from Shakespeare, Vaughan and Milton to Yeats, Eliot, and Kavanagh.
17. 'Filling in the Background: T.S. Eliot and Emily Dickinson.' From no. 16. An analysis of Eliot's 'A Song for Simeon' and Dickinson's 'I felt a Funeral, In My Brain.'
18. 'A Note On Oliver Goldsmith.' Introduction to *The Deserted Village*. Goldsmith Press: Newbridge 1974. Reprinted 1978, 1987. Argues that Goldsmith is 'an *Irish* writer, quintessentially so,' that he was well served by his 23 years in the Irish Midlands, and that he was dependent on his roots — a view which throws light on Egan's increasing awareness of the importance of locality in the realization of one's potential (cf. Nos. 1 and 5). Notes that in 'The Deserted Village,' which 'is full of energy and joy,' 'so soon after Pope and Dryden, and years before Wordsworth, Goldsmith has learned to write in simpler language about simple things.' Cf. also 'At the Birthplace of Oliver Goldsmith' in no. 10, 41-44.
19. 'Brian Bourke: Marcel Marceau from the Wings.' Introduction to a Portfolio, 1975. Argues that the best work of this distinguished Irish painter, which includes those drawings of the French mime artist Marcel Marceau, 'shows an extraordinary ability to get out of the way of what he draws or paints and allow it to have its own say.' Also suggests that Bourke transcends recording a mime artist to achieve an intimation into 'life itself, its exits and its entrances.'
20. 'Poetry and Politics: Yannis Ritsos.' Introduction to *Corridor and Stairs*. Dual-language collection of poems by Ritsos, translated by Nikos Germanakos. Goldsmith Press: Newbridge 1976. Argues that Ritsos is a great poet, who 'eulogises not only the spirit of resistance to tyranny but also, perhaps, the human spirit itself, discovering its roots, searching for its freedom.' Also emphasizes in his characteristic mixture of passion and understatement, Ritsos' place in the great Classical Greek tradition.
21. 'Some Thoughts on Ezra Pound.' *Era* 3 (1976). Notes on Pound's humor, final silence, and sense of joy, together with a more extended treatment of Fenollosa's article on the Chinese ideogram, which argues that modern English prose is in decline, one pointer being 'over-use of the verb "to be."'
22. 'Hermann Broch's *The Death of Virgil*,' *Era* 4 (1979). Asserts that the 'The novel's confrontation with ultimate questions moves, as true philosophy does, into the realm of poetry.'
23. 'W.H. Auden: A Carnival of Intellect?' Talk given on R.T.E. radio, November 1983. Argues that Auden 'never managed that body of great poetry which he seemed destined to do' and that his dilemma was 'a failure to integrate the personality.'
24. 'The Room Upstairs: Poetry in Modern Society.' Talk given on RTE radio, August 1984. Argues for a more imaginative attempt to interest people in poetry and against State patronage. Blames modern poets for losing their audience.
25. 'Máirtin O Direáin.' Talk for the launching of O Direáin's *Selected Poems/Tacar*

Dánta, Dublin, November 1984. Regards O Direáin as 'not only the finest Irish poet, writing in Irish, of our times; but more: the very embodiment of that Irish civilization and ethos, that precious *culture* which has now become a threatened species.' O Direáin, who died in 1989, was a friend of Egan.

26. 'Meeting Beckett'. Talk on RTE radio, April 1984. Recounts Egan's first meeting with Beckett in Paris in January 1984 (also in the poem 'Echo's Bones', no. 10, 13-14, which apostrophizes '— you Sam our navigator our valiant necessary/wanderer to the edges of this interpreted world').

27. 'The Bard of Athlone: John McCormack (1884-1945).' Delivered at the Opening of the John McCormack Centenary Exhibition, Athlone 1984. Praises McCormack's voice, diction, timing, and breath control, and finds that 'the Irish midlands are there in McCormack's singing.' Cf. 'Listening to John McCormack' in no. 10, 15.

28. '*A lack of Beauty in Our Lives:* James McKenna's Achievement.' Introduction to *James McKenna, A Catalogue of his Work* (Goldsmith Press: Newbridge 1985). Finds in regard to MacKenna's *Resurgence* in Limerick that 'The technique, the fineness, the virtuosity of McKenna's sculpting here as elsewhere speaks for itself. This magnificent piece radiates with energy, with inventiveness . . . *Resurgence* lays claim to being the finest public monument in modern Ireland.' Also writes of MacKenna as playwright and as poet.

29. 'Poetry and the Abyss.' Lecture given at The European Poetry Festival, Louvain. Published in the Festival Programme, Louvain 1986. Magisterial survey of how poetry in English treats the Abyss, *le gouffre.* Argues that the modern sense of the Abyss begins with the Romantics, that 'the two great laureates of unease' in the Victorian period are Hopkins and Dickinson, and that in the twentieth century 'it would certainly seem from the evidence of literature alone that the experience of the *abyssos* has become more anguished, more all-inclusive perhaps than ever before.'

30. *Poetry and Translation.* Paper for the Struga Poetry Festival. Published in the Festival Programme, Yugoslavia 1986. Also in *Studies* 76 (1987), 227-34. Asserts that translation *is* possible, and, flying in the face of Robert Frost's dictum, asserts that Poetry 'consists of that essence which can be translated.' Egan would wish a translator to be humble: he is against new metaphors and the notion of rhyme at all costs; he is for the translator 'making the other poet's world somehow his own'. Egan praises some translations of Pound, Beckett, and Roy Campbell.

31. 'The Poetry of Patrick Kavanagh.' From *Patrick Kavanagh, Man and Poet* (U.S.A. 1986, Ireland 1987). Rightly maintains that Kavanagh, as opposed to the ever ritualistic Yeats, 'reintroduced into Irish poetry the world of the *ordinary*.' Provocatively finds in Kavanagh 'a sensuous richness unequalled in English verse since John Keats,' regards him as 'one of the great religious poets,' and, most tendentiously of all, asserts that 'for me Patrick Kavanagh more and more seems the most gifted, the most important, the most necessary Irish poet of this century. Bar none.' For a full discussion of all of this see Arkins, Chapter Two: Backgrounds.

32. 'Peter Connolly.' *The Furrow*, June 1987. A tribute to the man who taught Egan at St. Patrick's College, Maynooth, where he was Professor of English (he died in 1987). After surveying the quality of Connolly's criticism, Egan concludes that 'He had a formidable intelligence and an equally daunting range of reference, right across

the spectrum of European and of American literature.' Calls for a collection of Connolly prose to be made — and the article sparked the publication of a Connolly book (from which, incredibly, Egan's article is missing!).

33. 'Thucydides and Lough Owel: The Greek Influence.' The Margaret Heavey Memorial Lecture, University College, Galway, 1988. A brilliantly succinct account of Greek literature and art. Singles out the facets of simplicity; clear-eyed truthfulness; human nobility; passion and control. Asserts 'I have always felt a special affinity with things Greek, with the literature and the language, the art, myths, and general mystique.'

34. 'The Death of Metaphor.' Lecture at The European Poetry Festival, Louvain 1988. Published in the Festival Handbook. Argues that modern poets, dispensing with metaphor in the face of chaos, 'tend to focus on the detail, on the objective thing, and to make it present in words, as vividly and completely as possible; speaking for itself.'

35. 'A Word on Ezra Pound.' *Paideuma* (forthcoming). Asserts that 'few poets manage in a lifetime to achieve such completeness of expression; no poet — I dare say — has developed so flexible a technique for rendering the complex of responses we call an experience.' Asserts also that 'Pound's *Cantos* do finally achieve an epic grandeur. Our peculiarly Twentieth Century equivalent of the epic: a fragmented civilization emerging from the rubble carrying its torn flag.'

36. 'Roderic O'Conor, an Irish Artist.' *Art and Antiques* (forthcoming). Argues that the depiction of woman by this Irish painter 'seems peculiarly Irish: a mixture of sensualist and puritan.' Argues further that 'No other Irish painter matches O'Conor in his capacity both to feel and to understand, to transcend. Obsessed and detached: a true artist.'

37. 'The Writer and Religion.' *Irish Writers and Religion*, edited by Robert Welch (Colin Smythe: Gerrards Cross 1990). Argues that in the face of modern chaos 'The religious impulse will always reveal itself as a search for wholeness, as a concern about one's roots, a longing for psychological and cultural individuality.' Asserts that 'In spite of his pessimism, Beckett's work asserts the life force.'

38. 'Hobbyhorses.' Unpublished. Includes material from nos. 19, 21 and 22. Also deals with the Vietnam War Monument in Washington, D.C.; Egan's Desert Island books; Singing and Plato; Comedy or Tragedy; The Use of the Verb 'To Be'; Music and Spontaneity; Two Kinds of Poetry; Music; and Traditional Irish Music.

39. *The Death of Metaphor — Selected Prose.* Colin Smythe: Gerrards Cross 1990/ Kavanagh Press: Newbridge/Barnes and Noble: Totowa, N.J. Contains all of nos. 17 to 38, with the sole exception of nos. 27 and 38. The prose of a major poet is always of great interest and especially when he writes about poetry and poets. Here Egan offers perceptive insights into poetry's relationship with politics and religion with the contemporary world and translation, as well as excellent criticism of a wide spectrum of poets from Goldsmith and Keats to Ritsos and O Direáin. Of particular note are the comments on two poets admired by Egan, Pound and Kavanagh, a combination that stresses his devotion to both local and international. Also noteworthy is the brilliant essay on the Greeks and the essays on the Irish visual artists O'Conor and McKenna.

40. Review of Hugh Kenner, *A Sinking Island:, The Modern English Writers* (London 1989). Endorses Kenner's trenchant attack on what passes for literature in Britain at the moment. Specifically stresses the limitations of Auden, the anti-intellectualism of Larkin. Champions Basil Bunting, whose 'Briggflats' is 'the finest sustained long poem since "The Waste Land."'

II. Translations of Desmond Egan

41. Japanese: *Paper Cranes*, Selected Poems of Desmond Egan translated and edited by Akira Yasukawa. To be published in Osaka in 1993. Contains 47 poems.

42. French: *Terre et Paix*. By Desmond Egan. Poèmes choisis et presentés par Patrick Rafroidi. Presses Universitaries: Lille 1988. This dual language book contains a total of 47 poems, which offer the French reader a representative sample of Egan's work from 1972 to 1989. The translations are by four people: Danielle Jacquin of the University of Lille (14 poems); Christine Pagnoulle of the University of Liege (17 poems, together with 4 in collaboration); the late Patrick Rafroidi of the Sorbonne (7 poems, together with 1 in collaboration); and David Scheinert, poet, novelist and playwright (7 poems, together with 3 in collaboration). The method of these translators is, as far as possible, to match Egan's original *vers libre* line for line. This works extremely well and provides translations that are not only accurate, but also of a very high standard. In addition, Rafroidi contributes a short, general introduction and specific introductions to the various books.

43. French: *Chanson pour mon Père*. Translated and edited by Jean Paul Blot. To be published in France in 1993. French version of *A Song For My Father*.

44. Dutch: *Echobogen*. Translated with an Introduction (see no. 65) by Peter Nijmeijer. European Poetry Festival Editions: Louvain 1990. Contains 50 poems in a dual-language presentation by one of Holland's best translators and includes poems from no. 11, *Peninsula*. Nijmeijer stresses Egan's ability to combine 'experience rooted in a personal Ireland with a genuinely international outlook: the touchstone of great poetry.'

45. Greek: *Selected Poems*. Translated by Kalliopi Rapanaki. In progress.

46. Italian: *Quel Sole Storno Che Gelido Passa — Poesia di Desmond Egan*. Selected poems translated and introduced by Giuseppe Serpillo, with other translations by Mary Pound-de Rachewiltz, who also contributes a Memoir, Rosalba Spinalbelli, Dr. Rizzardi and Rosangela Barone. Solfanelli 1992.

47. Swedish: *Selected Poems*. Edited and translated by Birgit Bramsbäck Leif Sjöberg (see no. 61) and Osten Sjöstrand. In progress.

48. Irish: *Tacar Dánta/ Selected Poems*. Translated and edited by Michael Hartnett, with other translations by Douglas Sealy, Gabriel Fitzmaurice, Tomás Mac Síomóin and Desmond Egan. Contains 36 poems in dual-language presentation. To be published by Forest Books, London.

49. Spanish: *Poemas Escogidas di Desmond Egan*. Translated and introduced by Pilar Gomez Bedate. Contains some 40 poems in dual-language presentation. To be published by Olifante, Madrid, in 1993.

50. German: *Selected Poems*. Translations by the distinguished German Eva Hesse; with Ditte König and Giovanni Bandini. In progress.

III. Interviews with Desmond Egan

51. A Conversation With Desmond Egan. Richard Paczynski. *Stylus*, Boston (1983). Paczynski asserts that Egan 'effuses an honesty of emotion that is almost unsettling.' Egan notes that memory plays 'a very important role' in the creation of poetry; that he is keenly interested in three types of music: classical, jazz, Irish traditional; praises the songs in James MacKenna's play *The Scatterin*'; argues for a presentation of poetry that would allow for larger audiences; regards Berryman as 'the most exciting and interesting American poet of the last generation' (cf. 'For John Berryman,' no. 8, 49-50).

52. Interview With Desmond Egan. Kevin T. McEneaney. As yet unpublished. Egan argues against punctuation in poetry; acknowledges his debt to the Greeks, especially the epigram, Sophocles' *Philoctetes*, and Thucydides; also to the 'direct and honest approach' of Kavanagh; and to the Spanish poets Lorca and Machado; tells us that 'Music continually runs through my head'; that the notion of two texts in *Seeing Double* (no. 7) came 'from painting'; that he admires Greek, Byzantine, Gothic, and modern American art; discusses his poetic development.

53. Tips for Writers. Desmond Egan interviewed by Brian Arkins. *Young Citizen* (September 1988), 12. Egan states that poetry today must engage with *both* public *and* private themes; that as regards the things that formed him 'music and painting were most important than writing'; attacks pop music as 'not firmly rooted in a specific cultural context'; advises young writers to be honest, allow for humor, and concentrate on content *rather* than form, suggesting that they not put all their energy into rhyming — which can be dispensed with.

54. Q. & A. With Desmond Egan. Anthony Roche. *Irish Literary Supplement* 8, 2 (Fall 1989), 22-23. Egan asserts in regard to the Midlands as a poetic topic 'I had to discover it, nearly invent it'; that 'reality is greater than words' and that the device of a dual text attempts to deal with that problem; 'it's the business of poetry to give a human spirit a voice'; regards lack of political engagement by Irish poets as 'a failure of contemporary Irish writing'; views Pound's *Cantos* as 'the only serious effort to write an epic in the 20th century'; argues that Beckett 'affirms life in the face of an extraordinary sense of meaningless, of chaos,'

55. Thucydides and Lough Owel: Interview With Desmond Egan. Brian Arkins. *Etudes Irlandaises* 14, 2 (1989), 117-20. Egan argues that poetry attempts to bridge the gap between the material world and the transcendent world of the Good; acknowledges his great interest in and debt to music and painting; attacks the abuse of language in contemporary prose; admires Kavanagh because of his 'concept of the parochial taking on universal relevance'; also the Greek language which is 'an incredibly supple system of communication'; argues that 'it is possible to translate'; admits that to him poetry is 'an obsession.'

56. Craft Interview With Desmond Egan. William Packard. *The New York Quarterly* 39 (Summer 1989), 33-53. Egan states that the American poetry he has liked best is

poetry 'with a sense of roots, which you get in Berryman and Ezra Pound'; that he is becoming more classical in the sense of 'pared-down to the simple and austere'; that the modern era is in many ways more confused and chaotic than the past; that Lowell's work *Notebooks* is 'pastiche Berryman' and that Lowell has been overrated; argues in favour of a united Ireland: 'the British flag should not be flying in Ireland'; criticises American foreign policy in Central and South America; asserts that his favourite prose book is Thucydides' *History of the Peloponnesian War*; that contemporary British poetry is 'in a very bad state indeed'; that Pound 'changed the whole course of twentieth century writing.'

57. *Te Weinig Vrede*. En interview met Desmond Egan. Peter G.W. van de Kamp. Egan attacks Irish literary cliques; expresses his affinity with Beckett; asserts that poetry must mirror the times; that Pound has been an influence on his technique; that he owes more to painting and music than to literature; praises Kavanagh's 'direct athletic confrontation with his themes'; rejects punctuation in poetry; refers to his own increasing concern with politics; sees the origin of the Northern Ireland problem in the plantations of Ulster and criticizes discrimination against Catholics.

57a. Interview with Desmond Egan. Sebastian Knowles. In *Learning the Trade: Essays on W.B. Yeats and Contemporary Poetry*, ed. D. Fleming. Locust Hill Press, U.S.A. 1992.

IV. Extended Critical Articles On Desmond Egan

58. Peter R. Connolly, Review of Egan's *Collected Poems* (no. 8). *Studies* 75 (Spring 1986), 102-05. The first substantial piece of criticism. Asserts that this volume 'affords ample evidence that another poet of considerable substance and stature has been around in Ireland for some time — having come to maturity about five years back.' Notes Egan's distinctive technique (lower case, non-capitals, no punctuation). Finds his voice tone and rhythms 'more American that British.' Asserts in regard to Ledwidge and Kavanagh that 'already Egan has invoked and surpassed these two tutelary spirits of his region.' Sees *Siege!* (no. 3) as a watershed in Egan's career, stressing its concern with public issues and anticipation of the later political poetry. Notes Egan's 'dual allegiance to the cosmopolitan and the local.' Explains the function of the sub-text 'as parallel or counterpoint, as parody or homage to the main poem.'

59. Conor Johnston, 'The Passionate Transitory in the Collected Poems of Desmond Egan.' *The Massachusetts Review* 29, 1 (Spring 1988), 149-68. Begins with a survey of Egan's career. Citing Kavanagh's phrase 'the passionate transitory,' asserts that Egan is preoccupied with this, with 'the passing of time, loss and death.' Proceeds to a volume by volume analysis of nos. 1-7. Notes in *Midland* (no. 1) a 'desire to freeze moments in time.' Finds that in *Leaves* (no. 2) 'Egan's approach to the passing of things becomes more personal.' Rightly regards *Siege!* (no. 3) as 'about the loss of an ideal,' that of modern Ireland. Finds that in *Woodcutter* (no. 4) 'Egan both laments what is passing and recognizes that he can't go home again.' Asserts re: *Athlone?* (no.

5) that 'one of the major successes in this volume lies in the manner in which Egan brings to life his boyhood responses to the town-world around him.' Notes that in *Snapdragon* (no. 6) there is 'a strong concern with loss or the possibility of loss.' Stresses Egan's commitment in *Seeing Double* (no. 7) to concrete, everyday things that are of necessity fragile and transitory.

60. Augustine Martin, 'Desmond Egan: Universal Midlander.' *Etudes Irlandaises* 13, 2 (1988), 81-84. Analyses the 'Introduction' to *Collected Poems* (no. 8) and finds the poet cannot stop a scavenging dog 'because he recognises himself in the animal, scavenging for insight between man and nature, present and future, impervious if not indifferent to society's disapproval.' Notes in *Midland* (no. 1) 'the particularity of landscape with its human imprint, its accretions of history.' Asserts that the poems in *Leaves* (no. 2) are 'more private, intense, introspective.' Argues that *Siege!* (no. 3) 'captures the uncertainty, tension, the confused motives and casual brutality of the occasion.' States in regard to Egan 'One of his masters is Ezra Pound whose open form and polyglot allusiveness he uses to remarkable effect.' Finds that Egan shares with Kavanagh 'a sensuous feeling for nature, especially for its humbler, intimate manifestations.' Asserts that Egan's voice 'will be heard with increasing attention and respect in the years to come.'

61. Leif Sjöberg, 'Desmond Egans Positioner.' *Artes* 6 (1988), 31-38. A general introduction in Swedish to Egan's work. Writes of Egan's flexible technique, wide range, and modernity. Refers to musical influence from classical *Lieder* to American jazz, including Irish traditional. After a short biographical sketch, talks about Egan's interest in international politics. Adverts to Egan's rejection of symbolism in his poem 'Non-Symbolist' (no. 8, 216-17), to his interest in Kavanagh's intense directness — a quality in evidence in 'Not on the Course' (no. 8, 133) — and to various parallels between Egan and Kavanagh. Talks about humor as a strand in Egan's poetry. Notes that Ezra Pound makes for another, unlikely, mentor. Sjöberg finishes an impressive and wide-ranging article by extolling the sensitivity of Egan's poetic technique.

62. Farah Mebarki, 'The Poetical World of Desmond Egan: A Poetical Osmosis Between In- and Out-Scapes'. Master's thesis directed by Patrick Rafroidi and presented to the Université de Paris 3 (Sorbonne Nouvelle), 1989. The main argument is that 'Egan endeavours to make his inside world melt into the outside universe and vice versa, to perform a kind of osmosis between both worlds.' This thesis is particularly good on the technical aspects of Egan's poetry: his command of various registers of English and of other languages; his similes and metaphors; his use of the sub-text; his neologisms, use of typography, links between poems. Further, it stresses Egan's political commitment, his love of nature, strong religious sense, interest in music and art. Provides a thorough account of Egan's basic landscape, the Irish Midlands, and of other landscapes he describes. Asserts that Egan 'has progressed from introspectiveness towards what may be called "extrospectiveness."' Notes that his philosophy of art 'is a kind of poetical faithfulness to reality,' and that 'The quest for eternity is a basic theme in Egan's poetry.'

63. Christine Pagnoulle, '*Seeing Double* and Feeling Far: The Poetry of Desmond Egan.' *Etudes Irlandaises* 14, 2(1989), 103-16. Comments on and quotes in full the poems 'Brother Sister Chile' (no. 10, 36-37); 'Hiroshima' (*ibid*, 22); 'Germany' (*ibid*. 46-47); 'Hitchhiker' (no. 8, 190-91); 'Young Gifted — and Unemployed' (no. 10, 11-12);

section III of 'A Song For My Father' (*ibid.*, 51-52); 'Have Mercy on the Poet' (*ibid.*, 40); 'Non Symbolist' (no. 8, 216-217). Notes that Egan 'insists upon poetry telling about the world in its immediacy, upon the essential mystery of things as they are, upon vision arising from concrete occurrences and experiences.' Finds in *A Song For My Father* (no. 10) a significant mixture of very personal and very public poems. Regards 'Young Gifted — and Unemployed' as 'a little *tour de force* of impersonation.' Argues that the sequence 'A Song For My Father' is not only confessional, but also 'truly universal.'

64. Peter G.W. van de Kamp, 'Desmond Egan.' In *Post-War Literature in English*, eds. T. d'Haen, J. Duytschaeuer et al. (Wolters-Noordhoff: Groningen 1989), 1-15. Notes the paradox that Egan is 'one of the least anthologised, yet most widely translated, contemporary Irish poets' and that Egan insists that 'the universal is of Irish, and the Irish of universal importance.' Writes of Egan's 'uncompromisingly modern style.' Argues that 'Like Yeats, Egan writes books, rather than individual poems.' *Leaves* (no. 2) is 'dominated by imagism' and characteristic by a melancholy and nostalgia.' In *Siege!* (no. 3) 'the unifying image (is) giving way to a mode of winter, of cynical fragmentation and tell-tale paradox and juxtaposition.' Argues that in *Athlone?* Egan embraces the local. Notes the mixture of political and personal poems in nos. 10 and 7.

65. Peter Nijmeijer, 'Intending' (Introduction) to no. 44. Strongly emphasizes Egan's native town of Athlone, including the humor of the inhabitants, and notes Egan's insistence in the poem 'Athlone?' on the local influence upon him. But also finds that the noteworthy phrase 'horizon afternoon' from the poem 'Midland' places Egan in the wider European tradition from the very beginning. Notes the American tone of Egan and the influence of Pound. Refers to the paintings of Francis Bacon which present a sitter from various angles within the one frame: this technique corresponds to the device of the sub-text. Quotes Egan (no. 54, 22): 'It's the business of poetry to give the human spirit a voice.' Stresses variety of theme in Egan's later work.

66. Patrick Rafroidi, 'Pilgrim's Progress' in *Irish Writers and Religion*, ed. Robert Welch. Colin Smythe: London 1990. Wonders at Egan's reticence, though a Catholic, at treating directly with religious themes. Is there any 'Catholic' literature in Ireland? In Egan there is not theorizing, only an over-all attitude which emerges from various scattered inferences. Enumerates these, choosing 'Peace' (no. 10, 38-39) as a fine example of a genuinely integrated religious poem, contrasting it with 'Requiem' (no. 8, 77) which is viewed 'a very fine Pagan poem.' Egan's later work continues to be Christian rather than 'Catholic,' more concerned with human values than with Catholic orthodoxies.

67. Brian Arkins, 'Too Little Peace: The Political Poetry of Desmond Egan.' In *Irish Writers and Politics*, edited Masaru Sekine (Colin Smythe: London 1990). Argues that Egan's political poems vigorously attack the injustice of corrupt dictatorships; emphasise the disastrous effects of this injustice on the individual person; acknowledge, particularly in regard to Ireland, the ambiguities of political situations; and use language that is, at all times, radically defamiliarizing. Provides detailed analyses of all of Egan's political poems — including 'Poems for Northern Ireland' (no. 1, 38-42), the volume *Siege!* (no. 3), and the following poems from *A Song For My Father* (no.

10): 'For Bejamin Moloise,' 'Hiroshima,' 'Brother Sister Chile,' 'Peace,' and 'Feed the World.' Concludes that these poems exhibits a striking *range* of treatment: imagist, epigrammatic, and discursive poems about Northern Ireland; the emphasis on ambiguity and paradox in modern Ireland in the very impressive *Siege!*; the prophetic and angry tone of the Third World poems; the pathos of the Hiroshima poem; the wit of the Falklands poem (the last not yet published; text in Chapter Six).

68. Giuseppe Serpillo, 'Desmond Egan: Poet.' Introduction to no. 46. Asserts that Egan 'is a poet because, as F.R. Leavis has written, "his interest in his experience is not separable from his interest in words."' Yet each single thing is 'grasped in their incomparable oneness and at the same time as lasting symbols of their condition in our time, fragile and heroic, absurd and coherent, contingent and absolute.' Notes that in the political poems there are two types of eloquence: a public type proper to man as a social being, and a private type that affects the individual person. Comments on the technical side of Egan: typrography, no capitals, no punctuation; and regards the device of the sub-text as 'used with great originality and success.'

69. Hugh Kenner, 'Introduction,' *Selected Poems.* Creighton University Press (U.S.A.) 1992. Contrasting Yeats and Egan at the age of 51, asserts that 'Egan feels free to be accurate.' Stresses Egan's omission of punctuation. Notes that he is 'the first Irish poet to have broken free from the need to sound "Irish."' ' Finds Egan's English 'as curious as Homeric Greek.' Considers the device of the sub-text.

70. *Desmond Egan — The Poet and His Work.* Edited by Hugh Kenner. Northern Lights, U.S.A. 1990. An important collection of essays by an international line-up of distinguished academics and writers, edited by the leading authority on Modernist writing. Includes nos. 54, 56, 58, 59, 60, 61, 63, 66, 68, 69; and, in addition, the following 17 items — nos. 71-87.

71. Hugh Kenner. 'Introduction.' Analyses the complexity of the poem with two texts. Stresses the importance of little words, such as 'so' in 'Thucydides and Lough Owel.' Notes that Egan believes that Beckett 'affirms life,' that 'it is possible to translate,' and that 'the British flag should not be flying in Ireland.' Calls the book 'a draft of a map.'

72. Michael Sundermeier. 'A Garden of Original Sin and Grace: Desmond Egan's Sense of Place.' Finds that 'Egan's strongest poems are anchored firmly in these particularities of Irish life.' Analyses the complexities of Egan's poem 'At Hopkins' Grave, June 8th, 1989' (*Studies,* Spring 1990, 70) and concludes that 'Egan has presented him to us in his memorial poem as an emblem of the human struggle with the love of the troublesome garden in which humanity finds itself.'

73. Brian Arkins. 'Thucydides and Lough Owel: The Greek Connection.' Chapter Seven of this book.

74. Vivienne Abbott. 'How It Was: Egan and Beckett.' Quotes the correspondence between Egan and Beckett, with facsimiles of some of Beckett's trenchant letters. The last of these letters said 'Too tired to write. Best Wishes. Sam.'

75. Brian Arkins. 'A Major Poet'. A review of *A Song For My Father* (no. 10), regarded as being *both* parochial (in Kavanagh's approbatory sense of the term), *and* international. Asserts that Egan has finally married the local intensity of Kavanagh to the knowledge of Yeats.

76. Kevin T. McEneaney. 'The Affirmation of Interiority: Love.' Analyses the volume *Snapdragon* (no. 6), whose structure 'will move through the psychological sequence of loss, reaching out to engagement, celebration, and finally, affirmation.' Finds the poem 'Je t'aime' 'a *tour de force* that risks nonsense, failure, silence, a confusion of languages, to describe the heights love inflicts on lovers.' Notes that at the end of 'Dernier Espoir' 'the key is a word, *yes*, a Joycean *yes* that alludes to Molly Bloom's soliloquy in *Ulysses*.'

77. Danielle Jacquin. 'Polyphony.' Asserts that the device of two texts resembles 'certain medieval polyphonic songs where the different parts are sometimes differentiated on the level of both words and music.' Notes that 'the double voice brings about an unexpected rhythm: it challenges the reader who hesitates between verticality and horizontally, wavers between the Roman type and italics, trying to read both at once and wishing to get rid of usual linearity.'

78. Robert Welch. 'Intimacy: A Meditation.' Asserts that 'Manners means dividing cleanly, which is what the voice does all the time in Egan's poetry.' Finds in Egan 'a rigor of the mind as much as a decorum of the spirit.'

79. Michael Murphy. 'Reading Desmond Egan.' Murphy, who, with his fellow newscaster Eileen Dunne and Egan himself, has successfully read Egan's poems at various centres, analyses the complex challenges involved in reading the poems aloud. Rightly finds that in *Siege!* (no. 3) 'the truth be faced in all its ambiguity.' Asserts that *Peninsula* (no. 11) 'marks a brilliant advance on his *engagé* poems.'

80. Maurice Harmon. 'An Introduction.' Regards Egan as 'a modernist in that he avoids formal shapes, rhyme schemes, traditional prosody and fluencies of sound.' Finds in Egan 'a strong visual quality.' Writing of *Snapdragon* (no. 6), notes it seeks 'to reflect and define love's many moods through images drawn from nature.'

81. Sean MacBride. 'Poems for Peace.' Asserts that poets, other artists and ordinary people 'alone can pierce through the armored concrete ramparts that protect injustice and inhumanity' and so that 'I am glad that a poet of the stature of Desmond Egan and a group like AFRI have joined hands to remind us of "Brother Sister Chile," of Benjamin Moloise, and of Father Romano.'

82. Thomas McCarthy. 'Unorthodox Poetry.' Notes Egan's independence ('he holds no party card') originality and constant experimentation. Regards 'The Northern Ireland Question' as 'a gem of protest.'

83. Ronald Bayes. 'Social Justice Concern.' Finds Egan 'an individual of impressive intellect and aesthetic keeness'; also 'a Poundian, very much concerned with social justice.' Correctly asserts 'this scope is far beyond that of most of today's celebrated poets.'

84. James McKenna. 'On the Launch of *A Song For My Father*.' Finds Egan striving 'to bridge that gap between non-being and being in a perceptible world.' Asserts that 'the voice of a poet who has commitments to other than flash-point causes can be heard throughout this Collection, engaging, observant, and dealing with our foibles in his own mildly laconic style.'

85. Carroll F. Terrell. 'Crossing the Stillwater.' Describes the trip of the author, President of the National Poetry Foundation of America, to meet Egan in Boston, New York, and Washington, D.C., in 1983 and the presentation to Egan of the National

Poetry Foundation Award for 1983, when Hugh Kenner asserted that 'Desmond Egan is hospitable in a new way to the literary traditions of Europe and America — in a way no English poet is.' At a reading by Egan in Maine, Terrell prophesied that 'Desmond Egan will yet be evaluated as Ireland's greatest modern poet.'

86. An Annotated Bibliography of Desmond Egan. Compiled by Brian Arkins. Contains nos. 1-69 of this Bibliography.

87. The Desmond Egan Papers in Georgetown University, Washington, D.C. Processed by James Helminski. Details the holdings there of Egan's papers: 'the manuscripts and typescript drafts of the poems included in Egan's published collections up to 1983'; plus additional papers up to Summer 1990.

Notes

Chapter One

1. P.R. Connolly, reviewing the *Collected Poems, Studies* 15 (1986), 102 (=Kenner, 27): 'it afford ample evidence to confirm that another poet of considerable substance and stature has been around in Ireland for some time having come to maturity about five years back.'

2. Kenner, 181-82.

3. For details of these translations see the Annotated Bibliography, section II.

4. *Desmond Egan—The Poet and his Work*, ed. H. Kenner (Northern Lights, U.S.A. 1990). Referred to as Kenner.

5. Also in Kenner, 184-201.

6. B. Arkins, 'Thucydides and Lough Owel: Interview With Desmond Egan,' *Etudes Irlandaises* 14, 2 (1989), 117.

7. *ibid.*

8. P.G.W. Van de Kamp, 'Desmond Egan' in *Post-War Literature in English*, eds. T. d'Haen, J. Duytschaeuer *et al.* (Wolters-Noordhoff: Groningen 1989), 3.

9. P.R. Connolly, (note1) 105 (=Kenner, 30).

10. For this poem see A. Martin, 'Desmond Egan: Universal Midlander', *Etudes Irlandaises* 13, 2(1988), 81-82 (=Kenner, 15-19).

11. For Mallarmé see C.L. Campos, 'Symbolism and Mallarmé' in *French Literature and Its Background: 5. The Late Nineteenth Century*, ed. J. Cruickshank (Oxford 1969), 132-53.

12. For Yeats' Symbolism see R. Ellman : *Yeats—The Man and the Masks* (London 1965), Index, S.V. Symbolism.

13. A. Symons, *The Symbolist Movement in Literature* (London 1899).

14. For this process in Horace see S. Commager, *The Odes of Horace* (New Haven/ London 1962), 235-306.

15. OED, sv. Requiem.

16. Cf. Patrick Kavanagh, 'Canal Bank Walk' in his *The Complete Poems*, ed. P. Kavanagh (Peter Kavanagh Hand Press: New York/Goldsmith Press: Newbridge 1987), 294:

> Leafy-with-love banks and the green waters of the canal
> Pouring redemption for me, that I do
> The will of God . . . .

Chapter Two

1. SPr 143-51.

2. T.S. Eliot, *On Poetry and Poets* (London 1969), 262.

3. H. Bloom, *The Anxiety of Influence* (Oxford 1975). For comment see T. Eagleton,

Literary Theory — An Introduction (Oxford 1983), 183-85; R. Selden, *A Reader's Guide to Contemporary Literary Theory* (Brighton 1985), 93-94; C. Norris *Deconstruction: Theory and Practice* (London 1986), 116-25; D. Fite, *Harold Bloom: the Rhetoric of Romantic Vision* (Uni. Massachusetts Press 1985); P. de Bolla, *Harold Bloom — Towards Historical Rhetorics* (London 1988).

4. Bloom (note 3), 122.

5. Clarke, quoted in R.F. Garratt, 'Patrick Kavanagh and the Killing of the Irish Revival,' *Colby Literary Quarterly* 17, 3 (1981), 172.

6. For Kavanagh see Egan, SPr 21-39; Seamus Heaney, *Preoccupations — Selected Prose 1968-1978* (London 1980), 115-30; *id., The Government of the Tongue* (London 1989), 3-14.

7. Cf. Heaney (note 6, 1989), 9: 'Kavanagh gave you permission to dwell without cultural anxiety among the usual landmarks of your life.'

8. F.R. Leavis, *New Bearings in English Poetry* (Harmondsworth 1963), 67.

9. W.B. Yeats, *Essays and Introduction* (London 1961), 499.

10. T.S. Eliot, *Collected Poems 1909-1962* (London 1974), 13; 23; 27.

11. For economic history see esp. *Cantos* XLII-LXXI and for Byzantium *Canto* XCVI.

12. Patrick Kavanagh, 'The Hospital' in *Patrick Kavanagh — The Complete Poems,* ed. Peter Kavanagh (New York/Newbridge 1987), 280.

13. Respectively SF 18-19; CP 218; 187-88; 202; 26.

14. Patrick Kavanagh, *Collected Pruse,* 282.

15. Kavanagh (note 12), 238.

16. For this role of Callimachus see B. Arkins, *Latomus* 47(1988), 285-93.

17. B. Arkins, 'Thucydides and Lough Owel: Interview With Desmond Egan,' *Etudes Irlandaises* 14, 2(1989), 119.

18. Egan, SPr 39.

19. Montague, 'Under Ben Bulben,' *Shenandoah* 16, 4(1965), 22-23.

20. Matthews, 'Modern Irish Poetry: A Question of Covenants' in *The Crane Bag Book of Irish Studies,* eds. M.P. Hederman and R. Kearney (Dublin 1982), 383.

21. Ezra Pound, quoted in M.A. Bernstein, *The Tale of the Tribe: Ezra Pound and the Modern Verse Epic* (Princeton 1980), 139.

22. Kingsley Amis, quoted by Charles Tomlinson in *The Modern Age,* ed. B. Ford (Harmondsworth 1966), 458.

23. W. Cookson, *A Guide to the Cantos of Ezra Pound* (London 1985), xiv.

24. Louis MacNeice, *Modern Poetry* (London 1938), 198.

25. A. Roche, 'Q. and A. With Desmond Egan,' *Irish Literary Supplement* (Fall 1989), 23 (=Kenner, 175).

26. *ibid.*

27. Arkins (note 17), 117.

28. Cf. P.R. Connolly, Review of Egan's *Collected Poems* (1984), *Studies* 75 (Spring 1986), 102 (=Kenner, 27); 'It is, however, Egan's voice-tone and rhythms which I find more American than British.'

29. Private conversation with the author.

30. *Irish University Review* 17 (1987), 329.

31. Arkins (note 17), 118-19.

32. Unpublished 'Interview With Desmond Egan' by K.T. McEneaney.
33. Arkins (note 17), 118.
34. McEneaney (note 32), 3.
35. For O'Conor see SPr 129-31 and for McKenna SPr 136-41.
36. McEneaney (note 32), 3.

Chapter Three

1. For the Irish landscape see M. Cawley in *Irish Studies — A General Introduction*, eds. T. Bartlett, C. Curtin, R. O'Dwyer, G.O'Tuathaigh (Dublin 1988), 7-19.
2. Donagh McDonagh, 'Dublin Made Me,' *The Hungry Grass* (London 1947), 19.
3. Patrick Kavanagh, 'Kerr's Ass' in *The Complete Poems*, ed. Peter Kavanagh (New York/Newbridge 1987), 254.
4. A. Roche, 'Q. & A. With Desmond Egan,' *Irish Literary Supplement* (Fall 1989), 22 (=Kenner, 168).
5. P.R. Connolly, Review of Egan's Collected Poems (1984), *Studies* 75 (Spring 1986), 103 (Kenner, 29)
6. C. Johnston, 'The Passionate Transitory in the Collected Poems of Desmond Egan,' *The Massachusetts Review* 29, 1(1988), 152 (=Kenner, 77).
7. For this phrase see P. Nijmeijer, Introduction to *Echobogen* (Louvain 1990), 14.
8. B. MacMahon, 'Place and People into Poetry', in *Irish Poets in English*, ed. S. Lucy (Cork/Dublin 1973), 60.
9. *OED*, s.v. *perch*.
10. 'Faults of the nettle.'
11. Johnston (note 6), 161 (=Kenner, 86).
12. Roche (note 4), 22 (=Kenner, 169).
13. Kavanagh (note 3), 238; 294-95.
14. T.S. Eliot, *Collected Poems 1909-1962* (London 1974), 190.

Chapter Four

1. H. Vendler, 'Four Elegies' in *Yeats, Sligo and Ireland*, ed. A.N. Jeffares (Gerrards Cross 1980), 221.
2. Chénier.
3. The poems 'For Benjamin Molise' and 'For Father Romano on His 45th Birthday' are dealth with in Chapter Six.
4. Tennyson, 'In Memoriam,' II.
5. For Watters/O Tuairisc see M. Nic Eoin, *Eoghan O Tuairisc: Beatha agus Saothar* (Dublin 1988), with Review by P.O.'Leary, *Irish Literary Supplement* (Fall 1989), 26.
6. A. Titley, in *The Crane Bag Book of Irish Studies*, eds. M.P. Hederman and R. Kearney (Dublin 1982), 895. For an analysis of *Aifreann na Marbh* see M. MacCraith, *Léachtaí Cholm Cille* 17 (1987), 61-94.
7. For Yeats' Platonism see B. Arkins, *Builders of My Soul: Greek and Roman Themes in Yeats* (Gerrards Cross 1990), 24-69.

8. Catullus 101.10.

9. Interestingly, a line added to the first version of the poem, published in *Midland* in 1972, when it appeared in the *Collected Poems* of 1983.

10. A. Roche, 'Q. & A. With Desmond Egan,' *Irish Literary Supplement* (Fall 1989), 23 (=Kenner, 173).

11. M. Reck, 'A Conversation between Ezra Pound and Allen Ginsberg' in *Ezra Pound*, ed. J.P. Sullivan (Harmondsworth 1970), 354.

12. E.M. Cioran, *Drawn and Quartered* (New York 1983): 'What we have really grasped cannot be expressed in any way at all, and cannot be transmitted to anyone else, not even to oneself, so that we die without knowing the exact nature of our own secret.'

13. John 14:2.

14. For the priamel see W.H. Race, *The Classical Priamel from Homer to Boethius* (Leiden 1982) and *id., Classical Genres and English Poetry* (London 1988), 35-55.

15. Horace, *Odes* 3.30.1: *exegi monumentum aere perennius.*

16. Propertius 1.19.12.

Chapter Five

1. A. Martin, 'Inherited Dissent: The Dilemma of the Irish Writer,' *Studies* 54 (1965), 1-20.

2. Byron, *Don Juan*, Canto III, viii.

3. For Egan's love poetry see K.T. McEneaney in Kenner, 98-103.

4. James Liddy, *A White Thoughlin a White Shade* (Dublin 1987), 52.

5. A Roche, 'Q. & A. With Desmond Egan,' *Irish Literary Supplement* (Fall 1989), 22 (=Kenner, 171).

6. Burns, 'My Love is Like a Red Red Rose.'

7. OED, s.v. if.

8. Yeats, 'Broken Dreams'.

9. Catullus 8.4.

10. Tennyson, 'Locksley Hall.'

11. Pound, *Canto* XXXVI.

12. Catullus 68b.159.

13. Terence, *Andria* 555.

Chapter Six

1. Lecture on 'Poetry and Commitment,' delivered at the Sorbonne, Paris in December 1987.

2. For the concept of defamiliarization see T. Hawkes, *Structuralism and Semiotics* (London 1977), 62-73; R. Seldon *A Reader's Guide to Contemporary Literary Theory* (Brighton 1985), 8-11; R. Fowler, *Linguistic Criticism* (Oxford 1986), 39-52.

3. For this process see the articles by J.P. Thorne, *J.Linguistics*, (1965), 49-59; 5(1969), 147-50; *New horizons in Linguistics*, ed. J. Lyons (Harmondsworth 1975), 185-97.

4. Selden (note 2), 33-37.

5. A. MacIntyre, *After Virtue — A Study in Moral Theory* (London 1981).

6. John Fowles, *The Aristos* (Triad/Granada 1981), 9.

7. 'Why Are the British in Northern Ireland?' *Era* 5 (1980).
8. D. Fennell, *The State of the Nation* (Dublin 1983); V. Buckley, *Memory Ireland* (Penguin Books, Australia 1985).
9. T.W. Adorno, *Prisms* (Cambridge, Mass. 1981), 32. For comment see K.K. Ruthven, *Feminist Literary Studies — An Introduction* (Cambridge 1984), 32-34.
10. Lecture (note1).
11. Egan (note 7).
12. For Solzhenitsyn see, e.g., C. Booker, *The Seventies* (Harmondsworth 1980), 47-64.
13. Seorise Mac Thomáis, *An Blascaod a Bhí* (Maynooth 1977).
14. Egan (note 7).
15. F. Fanon, *Wretched of the Earth* (New York 1961).
16. T. Adorno and M. Horkheimer, *Dialectic of Enlightenment*, trans. J. Cumming (London 1979).
17. Saul Bellow, *The Dean's December* (Harmondsworth 1982).

Chapter Seven

1. This chapter has appeared in Kenner, 32-44.
2. Louis MacNeice, *The Strings Are False* (London 1982), 87.
3. S. Doubrovsky, quoted in J. Hawthorn, *Unlocking the Text* (London 1987), 27: (re literature) 'what it *says* achieves its full meaning through what it *does not say*; and that is precisely what it *means*.'
4. Yeats, 'Colonus' Praise.'
5. Translated by B. Arkins.
6. Louis MacNeice, *Autumn Sequel*, Canto VIII.
7. B. Arkins, *Builders of My Soul: Greek and Roman Themes in Yeats* (Gerrards Cross 1990), 170-72.
8. C.M. Kraay, *Archaic and Classical Greek Coins* (London 1976), 218-24.
9. R. Lattimore in *On Translation*, ed. R.A. Brower (New York 1966), 49.
10. Virginia Woolf, quoted in T. Savory, *The Art of Translation* (second ed., London 1968), 60.

Chapter Eight

1. E. Estyn Evans in *The Irish World*, ed. B. de Breffny (London 1977), 8.
2. For its antiquities see J. Cuppage, *Archaeological Survey of the Dingle Peninsula* (Ballyferriter 1986).
3. M. Cruise O'Brien in *The Pleasures of Gaelic Literature* ed. J. Jordan (Dublin/Cork 1978), 37.
4. E. Hussey, *The Presocratics* (London 1974), 40.
4a. Gallarus oratory may date from as late as the 12th century; Y.P. Harbison, *Mediaeval Archaeology* 14(1970), 34-59.
5. S.O. Tuama and T. Kinsella, *An Duanaire 1600-1900: Poems of the Dispossessed* (Mountrath 1981), 97.

6. For *The Islandman* see Cruise O'Brien (note 3), 25-38; John McGahern, *The Irish Review* 6(1989), 55-62. See also George Thompson, *An Blascaod a Bhí* (Maynooth 1977).
7. Cruise O'Brien (note 3), 26.
8. Quoted in Cruise O'Brien (note 3), 28.
9. For early modern Ireland c. 1500-1700 see N. Canny in *The Illustrated History of Ireland*, ed. R.F. Foster (Oxford 1989), 104-60. For Ireland and Elizabeth see R. Bagwell, *Ireland Under the Tudors*, 3 vols. (London 1963); C. Falls, *Elizabeth's Irish Wars* (London/New York 1970); N. Canny, *The Elizabethan Conquest of Ireland* (Brighton 1976).
10. For the Dún an Óir massacre see Bagwell (note 9), Vol. III, 69-78; Falls (note 9), 142-45; A. O'Rahilly, *The Massacre at Smerwick (1580)* (Cork/London 1938); G. O'Tuathaigh, *The Massacre at Dún an Óir 1580* (Ballyferriter 1980).
11. Falls (note 9), 144.
12. Edmund Spenser, *A View of the Present State of Ireland*, ed. W.L. Renwick (Oxford 1970), 107-08.
13. Renwick (note 12), 185-87.
14. O'Rahilly (note 10).
15. O'Rahilly (note 10), 34.
16. Bingham, quoted in O'Rahilly (note 10), 2.
17. For Raleigh in Ireland see D.B. Quinn, *Raleigh and the British Empire* (London 1962), 32-35.
18. P. Ure in *The Age of Shakespeare*, ed. B. Ford (Harmondsworth 1955), 144.
19. Raleigh, quoted by L.G. Salinger in Ford (note 18), 26.
20. *Nichomachean Ethics* 1139a 35.
21. Grey, quoted by O'Rahilly (note 10), 23-24.
22. Canny 1976 (note 9), 135.
23. Quoted in O'Rahilly (note 10), 6.
24. Renwick (note 12), 214.
25. For this poem of Spenser, *The Ruines of Time*, see W. Nelson, *The Poetry of Edmund Spenser* (New York/London 1965), 66-69.
26. Canny 1976 (note 9), 85-8.
27. Translated by B. Arkins.
28. See J. Culler, *Barthes* (Fontana 1983), esp. 33-35, 61-69.

INDEX

Index

Index